FINANCIAL INTELLIGENCE

FUNDAMENTALS OF PRIVATE PLACEMENT PROGRAMS

SIR PATRICK BIJOU

DESCRIPTION

I REVEAL THE SECRET THAT NO BANKER IS PREPAIRED TO DISCLOSE. This book helps you understand how private placement programs (PPP) works. It also discusses the various process and advantages of private placement programs, and shows you how you can put the knowledge to use. It also aims at describing how these programs work and understanding the two different types of programs. I am often contacted by project developers, investors, entrepreneurs, and brokers who are looking to raise capital, or who are looking for investment opportunities that provide higher returns for themselves or their clients. This initial inquiry often leads to a discussion of private placement programs and trade platforms. It describes extensively how best Private Placement Program Works and *as you read this book you'll discover:*

1. Private Placement Investment Program History
2. Private Placement Programs and Trade Platforms - What They Really Are
3. Private Placement Invest Debt Contracts Terms
4. Private Placement Market Lenders
5. Restrictions Affecting Private Placement
6. Who Are the Agents? The Role of Agents
7. Agent Operations under Rule 144A
8. Credit Crunch in the Private Placement Market

9. Private Placements: SCAM or REAL?
10. And More.

Once you have a clear understanding of what investing in these programs involve and how fractional reserve banking comes into play, you will discover the path into investments into these lucrative but secretive opportunity.

ABOUT THE AUTHOR

Sir Patrick is an eclectic writer, lives in the United Kingdom and was born in 1958 in Georgetown and raised in London, England.

His diverse writing prowess has been influenced by many experiences.

He pursued several courses of study at several universities, and declared two majors during his schooling which included the areas of Business and Economics and finally obtained his doctorate in Economics and International banking.

In all these scholastic studies though, the true treasures he took away are not the certificates (though those are very important), but instead the experiences he had, the people he met, the foods he ate and even the places he stayed.

"In truth, I am a citizen of the world and this greatly influences my writing.

So, if you are already a fan of mine, I appreciate you. If you are not yet one, then what are you waiting for? Read a book and then read some more. I create characters that resonate with you and infuse life into all I write".

Finding my Books

Sir Patrick has written over 15 published fictional and non-fictional books across several genres, I have realized the need to make it easier for my readers to find my books.

I would appreciate if you would be kind enough to leave a review of this book.

TABLE OF CONTENTS

INTRODUCTION

Before tackling the topic, it is important to understand the basic reasons for the existence of PPP's. This document explains the core concept of what money is and how it is created; controlling the demand for money and credit, and the process of issuing a debt note; discounting the note, and selling and reselling it in arbitrage transactions - and how all this leads to exceptional profits, often used for major project or (private) corporate financing.

The private placement program is an important source of long-term funds for U.S. corporations. Between 1987 and 1992, for example, the gross volume of bonds issued in the private placement market by nonfinancial corporations was more than 60 percent of that issued in the public corporate bond market. Furthermore, at the end of 1992, outstanding privately placed debt of non- financial corporations was more than half as large as outstanding bank loans to such corporations.

Despite its significance, the private placement program has received relatively little attention in the financial press or the academic literature. This lack of attention is due partly to the nature of the instrument itself. A private placement is a debt or equity security issued in the United States that is exempt from registration with the Securities and Exchange Commission (SEC) by virtue of being issued in transactions "not involving any public offering." Thus, information about private transactions is often limited, and following and analyzing developments in the market are difficult. The last major study of the private placement market was published in 1972, and only a few articles have appeared in economics and finance journals since then.

This study examines the economic foundations of the market for privately placed debt, analyzes its role in corporate finance, and determines its relation to other corporate debt markets. The market for privately placed equity is briefly described in appendix B. In the remainder of the study, the term private placement refers only to privately placed debt.

There seem to be two widespread misperceptions about the nature of the private placement program. One is the belief that it is mainly a substitute for the public bond market: that is, issuers use it mainly to avoid fixed costs associated with SEC registration, and lenders closely resemble buyers of publicly issued bonds. This misperception may have arisen because private placements are securities and because the definition of a private placement focuses on its exemption from registration. Regulatory considerations and lower transaction costs do cause some issuers to use the private market. Principally, however, it is an information-intensive market, meaning that lenders must on their own obtain information about borrowers through due diligence and loan monitoring. Many borrowers are smaller, less-well- known companies or have complex financings, and thus they can be served only by lenders that perform extensive credit analyses. Such borrowers effectively have no access to the public bond market, which provides funding primarily to large, well-known firms posing credit risks that can be evaluated and monitored with publicly available information. In this respect, private market lenders, which are mainly life insurance companies, resemble banks more than they resemble buyers of publicly issued corporate debt. Even if registration of public securities were not required, something resembling the private placement market would continue to exist.

The second misperception is that the private placement market is identical to the bank loan market in its economic fundamentals. This misperception may have been fostered by the tendency of some recent studies of information- intensive lending to group all business loans not extended through public security markets under the rubric "private debt." Included in this category are bank loans, private placements, finance company loans, mezzanine finance, venture capital, and other kinds of nonpublic debt. A principal finding of this study, however, is that all information-intensive lending is not the same. In particular, the severity of the information problem that a borrower poses for lenders is an important determinant of the markets in which the company borrows and of the terms under which credit is available.

Besides dispelling these misperceptions, the study describes in detail the nature and operation of the private placement market. It also offers empirical support for the proposition that the private placement market is information intensive and that private market lenders and borrowers are different from lenders and borrowers in other markets. It provides a theoretical explanation for the existing structure of business debt markets that builds upon recent theories of financial intermediation, covenants, debt contract renegotiation, and debt maturity. Finally, it analyzes some recent developments in the private placement market, including a credit crunch, the effect of the SEC's Rule 144A, and changes in the roles that banks play.

A constant theme running through the global non-bank finance market as it has evolved since the 2008 crash, has been private placement programs (PPP's). Sadly, the whole sector has become tainted as unscrupulous individuals, with no real knowledge of how they operate, have persuaded the unaware to part with significant sums of money on the expectation that they were going to reap outstanding returns. So prevalent did these scams become that the FBI and other agencies actually put out warnings that these programs are, in themselves, a scam.

Blame the internet, it's the cause of much grief in the market generally! It's probably true to say that less than 1% of what's on offer on the internet is real. But nevertheless, PPP's are a genuine, private 'Tier-1' market place where financial instruments of many types (mostly MTN's) are transacted by independent traders and trading groups, operating across the world's top-tier banks. The market has operated successfully for seven decades.

This Guide is written with the intent of assisting those considering entering this market to make the right decisions. It explains some of the obscure or unclear aspects of PPP's and has been prepared from personal experience, and also plagiarizing content from papers produced by others who, because of the confidential and sensitive nature of these programs, prefer to remain anonymous.

CHAPTER 1

Private Placement Investment Program History

In the 1990s, the trading in bank instruments was and is presently a multi-trillion dollars industry worldwide. The World's largest fifteen to twenty-five Holding Companies of North American and European Banks are authorized to issue blocks of debt instruments such as medium-term notes, debenture instruments, and standby letters of credit at the behest of the United States Treasury for the United States Treasury Trust and Foundations and the United States Federal Reserve. The Instruments issued are backed by a Treasury undertaking.

The genesis of this marketplace was the 1945 Bretton Woods Conference of world's leaders. The principles originally championed as answers to post World War II economic stability are still the impetus for the operation of these transactions today These transactions started some fifty years ago, have grown and been continuously modified, and as described in this article are Private Placement U.S. Treasury and

Federal Reserve investment transactions administered by select Western Banks.

A short historical summary will help to understand the origin of these transactions and the reasons why the Treasury backed, private bank instrument marketplace has remained strong and viable notwithstanding the great social, political, and economic changes the world has experienced during the last half century.

With World War II having come to a close, the leading political and economic authorities of the world met in Bretton Woods, New Hampshire. Their purpose was to formulate a common plan to rebuild the war's massive devastation and to impose global restraints upon forces which had twice led to world chaos during the first half of the Twentieth Century and left economic collapse in its wake.

To accomplish this goal, these leaders sought to empower universally recognized international institutions capable of effectuating and preserving political order and capable of encouraging and facilitating world economic trade and cooperation. The World's leading economists advocated the establishment of an international banking system which administered a universally accepted "currency". It was believed that a centralized world authority, and a standard world currency, with fixed exchange rates among the various currencies of the world was the formula for the stimulation of universal economic growth and the maintenance of economic balance and stability though the economies of the world.

John Maynard Keyes urged the adoption of a standard currency. The political realities of Nation State's autonomy, however, inevitably precluded the adoption of a uniform currency. As an alternative, the international Leaders resolved to adopt the United States Dollar as the standard world currency for international trade. It was gold backed and the most stable currency. This adoption of the United States Dollar as the world's standard currency for international trade was the milestone which triggered the development of the bank instrument marketplace. The Bretton Woods Conference gave birth to the United Nations, the World Bank, the International Monetary Fund (IMF) and the Bank of International Settlements (BIS).

The World Bank was structured to function in a manner consistent with traditional commercial banks. It was created to act as lender to the poorer and less developed countries. Funding for the World Bank came from the assessment of the more industrialized countries. Today, it takes deposits from more than 140 member Governments and lends to the lesser developed countries in need of international capital.

The International Monetary Fund was created to work in conjunction with the World Bank. While the defined role of the IMF has been adjusted through the years, its basic purpose has remained the same: administer global economic stability and political harmony through targeted lending to member countries to facilitate growth, to maintain relative stability among the various world currencies and to avoid collapse in times of crisis.

Most of the world's economies experienced great post World War II expansion. With this expansion came increased international trade and the need for more and more United States Dollars to accommodate this growth. In permitting the U.S. Dollar to be adopted as the world's standard currency, the role of the United States Treasury and the United States Federal Reserve expanded.

To protect the dollar's value while increasing the dollar's availability, the Treasury commenced to work with the World Bank, the IME, the BIS and through the Federal Reserve, and the largest Western European Banks. They developed a system of issuing uniform financial bank instruments in U. S. Dollar denominations m accordance with the new and universally accepted financial standards. In doing so these U.S. Agencies and International Institutions merely incorporated the existing basic operating procedures of the major Western European Banks,

The United States banks manage their asset liability by offsetting short term deposits against long term loans while Western European banks fund their customers' long-term borrowing needs through the issuance of various bank financial instruments including Medium Term Notes and Letters of Credit. A plan was enacted to permit the Western European Banks to issue financial instruments in United States Dollar denominations pursuant to the expressed authority of the U.S. Treasury through the U.S. Federal Reserve. In enacting this system, the Treasury/Federal Reserve authorized the Western European Banks to capture the expatriated U.S. Dollars from the world marketplace and with the new credit created, issue these 'new" Dollars into circulation in specific geographical locations where investment was needed, over the controlled life of the instrument. The implementation of this system following the Bretton Woods Conference provided a means for the U.S. Treasury and Federal Reserve to control the rate and volume and placement location of the U.S. Dollars being introduced into the global marketplace.

In its attempt to further solidify the universal acceptance of the U.S. Dollar as the standard world currency, the Bretton Woods Conference had fixed the price of Gold backing the U.S. Dollar at $35.00 an ounce. During the 1950s and the 1960s the price of gold in the open market had increased to a price nearly ten times that amount. The need to back the U.S. Dollar with gold valued at $35.00 an ounce while simultaneously providing sufficient U.S. Dollars to accommodate the increased needs of the international marketplace created significant stress on the United States Monetary system. The United States did not have enough gold to continue issuing the dollars necessary to continue to support international economic expansion.

On August 15, 1971, facing a threatened speculative run on the U, S. gold reserves, President Richard Nixon renounced America's promise to convert paper dollars into gold upon demand. With this executive proclamation the United States abandoned the gold standard. In the absence of the gold backed standard currency the idea of fixed exchange rates among all currencies of the world became passe, and by 1973 the IMF., The World Bank and the Bank of International Settlements had abandoned the idea of fixed exchange rates.

Within the territorial limits of the United States the U.S. Federal Reserve exerts influence upon the domestic economic trends by the regulation of domestic bank reserve requirements and the adjustment of the Federal Discount Rate. While these may be internally effective tools, they are inadequate to provide the international control demand in the global marketplace. The United States Treasury expanded the roll of the Federal Reserve System to monitor the International markets separate and apart from domestic duties. In implementing the International System of world order, the United States Treasury through the Federal Reserve has the largest World Banks issue bank financial instruments in significant U. S. Dollar denomination. As these instruments are issued and sold the U. S. Dollars extracted from circulation and the new credit created in exchange for the new bank instruments, control over the Global U. S. Dollar money supply is affected. These transactions are meaningful because the bank instruments are of such significant dollar amounts that the effect of these sales will have a direct impact upon the volume of the U. S. Dollar in circulation within a particular local economic system. Once the Federal Reserve has collected in the Dollars, they can be reinserted into targeted segments of the global economy in accordance with the United States Treasury and the G¬8 Nations determined policies.

The same system is the foundation wherein the IMF discretely attempts to maintain world order. As economic, political, and social factors alter the relationships of the Nations of the World, the IMF is equipped to respond through the power of responsible administration of financial aid. Loans may be granted to member countries to fund various individual projects which are beneficial to its citizens and mankind in general. Should a Central Bank of an individual country run into a deficit in its balance of payments, the IMF is able to supply short term financing to a member country. Functioning in this manner, the IMP can interject an immediate fix to the short-term instability of an individual county white at the same time avoiding calamitous consequences to the other nations with whom the unstable country may have contracts.

A review of past events reveals the extent of the IMF's role as: The force behind the bailout of Mexico, the 10-Billion-dollar loan commitment to Russia, the attempts to bring stability to Africa and to undermine the oppressive authority of African Overlords, the industrial development of Eastern Europe, the reconstruction of Bosnia, and the development of free markets in South America.

However, these targeted loans come with definite strings attached. The funding of such loans maybe conditioned upon the country's demonstrating to the World Bank or the IMF officials that it has reduced its inflation rate, reduced its import tariffs, and opened its markets to external forces, ceased destroying its rain forest, terminated policies inconsistent with basic human rights, taken steps to eliminate corruption, cut internal spending in certain areas, adjusted objectionable internal policies, and is acting in accordance with universally recognized concepts of human dignity.

By the sale of Bank Instruments, the IMF is able to promptly respond to issues in a targeted fashion. This system avoids the need to submit requests to the various member counties for the use of politically budgeted funds and avoids the parochial, partisan, political processes of the parliaments of various Nation States.

The Bank of International Settlements (BIS) is a little-known private institution based in Basel, Switzerland. It also performs a critical function in the preservation of order in the global monetary system Control of this institution is actually vested in private individuals. Not governmental officials. The principal functionaries are the Private Central Bankers from the world's industrialized countries. Like the IMF, the Bank of International Settlements functions in the nature of a world economic security net and clearing house. It is capable of moving billions of dollars from one country to another to expeditiously correct potentially disruptive financial imbalances between countries, and to effectuate the prompt administration of financial first aid to individual Nations and financial institutions in major crisis situations. The BIS also helps maintain the relative stability of the world currencies as well as the global system as a whole.

The Medium-Term Notes are issued by the largest World Banks at the instructions and authority of the U.S. Treasury directly or through the Federal Reserve and distributed through the largest banks through a well- established private marketing system. This marketing system of Private Treasury Trading Trusts, Foundations and Federal Reserve Accounts, exclusively market these instruments and these accounts are administered by the participating bank. The proceeds generated by the sale of these instruments are retained by the U.S. Treasury or the Federal Reserve and reintroduced into the market place when deemed appropriate These funds may be used to fund loans made by the INIF to its member countries. By funding specific projects, the INIF can monitor the proceeds and certify that the funds are being used as agreed.

These Private Trading Entities regularly purchase these instruments on the initial issue or Primary market and the pricing is at a negotiated discount. The instruments are immediately sold to a well-defined private and discrete market at the market rate or at secondary market prices. This new profit is new credit created that can be used for financing of U.S. Treasury registered and Approved Projects. As indicated in the Federal Reserve Bulletin, Anatomy of the Medium-Term Note market," August, 1993 page 765, these transactions involve "riskless principal" as all of the instruments bought are sold prior to purchase.

In the Private Placement Program transactions, trading is conducted on the strength of the U.S. Treasury Department Approval of the holder of the funds after they have been shown to be good, clean and of non-criminal in origin. It is the value of the funds as evidenced to the Treasury Trust or Foundations, or the Federal Reserve, not the funds themselves that finance the purchase of the instruments by the participating Private Placement Transaction.

In the event that the instruments have been issued for a World Bank or IMF project, the funds are generated by the sale of the instruments by the Private Transaction Accounts and are available for use in funding the loan commitments made by IMF or other such international agency. The instruments are commonly five hundred million-dollar notes with a ten-year maturity bearing interest of seven-and one-half percent, back by a Treasury Instrument of like terms, and purchased at a discount and resold to major institutions at the market rates.

Through the implementation of this system the U. S. Treasury and the Federal Reserve cause dollars to be moved from one country to another in a fashion consistent with the economic and political policies of the G-8 + Nations, the United States Government, The World bank, The IMF, and the United Nations. In so doing the participants are able to effect foreign aid and the IMF is able to significantly fund their commitments without resorting to individual assistance from the treasuries of its member states.

The Private Transaction Accounts operate with a profit motivation and they may have Private Placement Participation from private individuals and other private entities which must be screened and cleared by the administering agencies. The Investment Manager Limited, provides private individuals and other private entities access to this market in the form of accepting deposits of Private Placement Funds. Entry requires The Investment Manager Limited to obtain a clearance and Approval of the Depositor, from the United States Treasury Department/Federal Reserve for each Private Placement Deposit. This process may be initiated by submitting necessary documentation including proof of good, clear clean funds on non-criminal origin together with the appropriate bank documentation. (The format of necessary documentation is available upon request).

The United States Treasury rules are applicable to all banks who have administration and distribution arrangements with the Treasury to do this business in U.S. Dollar denominations. Recent enactments by the U.S. Treasury have extended the application of these rules to all participating foreign banks issuing instruments in U. S Dollars as well as all domestic banks. Some of the limitations include: type of capital banks may use for such activities, the manner in which participating capital may be procured, the manner in which the profits can be divided and accounted for, and to whom and under what circumstances of this activity can be made.

The form of security offered to participants in the Private Placement Transaction will be assignable Deposit Receipts from the Custody Safekeeping Accounts of The Investment Manager Limited that hold the Private Placement Deposit. The Custody Safe Keeping Account will hold the cash deposit or securities equal to or of greater value than the original Deposit.

The Treasury rules have a broad impact upon the nature and scope of all bank's activities. Banks are precluded from using funds held on deposit within the institution for use in these transactions. The rules require that the participant be the legal owner of the funds and banks are prevented from soliciting clients and funds for participation in a trading transaction.

As a consequence of these restrictions and m response to the continual need for capital to initiate and complete Approved Projects, these transactions are established in a discreet, Private Placement Program Transaction which function as the Private Placement Transactions. To participate with a Private Placement Transactions the clearance of the participant and the depositor's funds by an authorized representative of the United States Treasury is essential. After the funds have been screened as good, clean, of non-criminal origin, and U. S. Treasury approval has been procured, the participant is in a position to place the funds in a Custody Safe Keeping Account or Corporate Account, at a nominated World Bank acceptable to the Depositor and The Investment Manager Limited.

The Treasury Approval is significant as it represents that the funds are clear and the approval is extended to the established Bank Account and authorized by the Treasury rules, it represents that disclosure about the details of the transaction my take place, it represents that the earnings on the deposited funds are legally exempt from the limits imposed upon banks pay out restrictions set by the U. S. Federal Reserve discount rate limitations, and it means that the bank may deliver to the Established Bank Account an Assignable Depository Receipt as security for the deposited funds.

A commonly offered security is that of a Deposit Receipt or an Assignment for the deposit hinds which is issued by the Established Bank Account of The Investment Manager limited through the Administering Bank, The Safekeeping Receipt or Assignment, is accompanied by limiting instructions in which the Administering Bank agrees to maintain a level of funds equal to the funds deposited or "A+" rated Bank or U. S. Treasury instruments equal or greater to the total of the deposited funds.

The Investment Manager Limited commits the value of the funds in the Custody Safe Keeping Account to a

Treasury Trust or Treasury Foundation Transaction Account, who administers ad of the trading that creates new credit for the financing of Approved Projects. New credit is created and generated by the repeated use of the value of the funds deposited to finance successive buy and sell transactions in the Treasury Transaction Accounts.

In February 1997, The Treasury Department issued new rules for the distribution of the new created credit and these rules are regularly being updated and amended.

The I. S. Treasury Department enforces all of theft rules to ensure compliance with their directives. This process is closely regulated through U. S. Treasury Compliance Officers who are assigned to audit the business activities of the various participants.

Understanding Private Placement

There are two kinds of private placement—preferential allotment and qualified institutional placement. A listed company can issue securities to a select group of entities, such as institutions or promoters, at a particular price. This scenario is known as a preferential allotment.

The eligibility of investors, in this case, is specified in Chapter XIII of SEBI (DIP) guidelines. Investors may have a lock-in period.

A company must take permission from its shareholders to carry on with preferential allotment.

Recently, the SEBI eased this norm of preferential allotment to help revive Satyam Computers.

Under qualified institutional placement, a listed company issues shares or convertibles to institutional buyers only. This norm is followed as per the provisions in Chapter XIIIA of SEBI (DIP) guidelines. The process encourages listed companies to raise funds from the domestic market rather than going to foreign markets.

we are often contacted by project developers, investors, entrepreneurs, and brokers who are looking to raise capital, or who are looking for investment opportunities that provide higher returns for themselves or their clients. This initial inquiry often leads to a discussion of private placement programs and trade platforms.

Private Placement Programs and Trade Platforms - What They Really Are

Trading Platforms are pools of capital that invest in a wide variety of financial instruments including stocks, bonds, commodities, ETF's and foreign exchange. These pools of capital may be a number of legal entities; however, the most common is known as a PPP, an acronym for Private Placement Programs. Private Placement Trading Programs are not offered to the general public. They are exactly what their name implies, offerings of membership interest to a select group of chosen investors who meet certain financial requirements.

The minimum investment in these Private Placement Programs can often be quite high and require a lockup period, where the capital is committed to the Trade Program for a certain amount of time. The minimum investment levels and principal commitment periods vary depending on the type of investments and the objective of the investment. One-year lock ups are not uncommon and in some investments the lock up period may be even longer. Lock ups serve a very important function. They provide the Trade Platform Managers and Platform Traders with time in which to obtain results for the investors. Platform Traders want to know that the capital allocations they have been given to trade are for a long enough period of time to allow a particular trading strategy time to mature.

If you were to look at the returns of outstanding Platform Traders you would see profitable results over time; however, in the short term they may have a period of negative returns. If your interest is in traders with no down periods, please read no further, as they do not exist, contrary to popular belief. There is no such thing as free money. Trading involves risk. Every investor dream of opening the door today and finding tomorrows Wall Street Journal, but this only exists in fantasy. Platform Trading requires hard work, tremendous discipline, patience, and superb talent The fact is very few people have the gifts to be a successful trader. The Platform Traders at the very top of their peers are rewarded with staggering wealth.

Platform Traders utilize many strategies to help determine profitable trades, such as macro analysis, price theory, fundamental analysis, value analysis and many more investment strategies. What superior and outstanding Platform Traders can do is make enough winning trades over time, irrespective of what strategy they may use to accumulate trading profits. However, a number of their trades will not be winners. A large part of successful Private Placement Program trading is risk management; controlling losses and preserving investment capital.

One of the very basic risk management techniques utilized by Private Placement Program Traders is only risking a very small percentage of the investment capital on every trade. It is usually between one half and two percent on a particular trade. If a trade loss hits a defined percentage allocation, the trade is closed out. The average investor has an extremely difficult time taking a loss. In fact, it is a human tendency to hold on to losing trades and cut winning trades short, which is the very opposite of what great Platform Traders do. Risk management systems can get very complex and Platform Traders often write complex algorithms to manage risk when there are many positions and trade strategies running all at once.

The advent of the computer has radically revolutionized trading, just as it has every facet of our lives. Modern Trading Platforms are heavily dependent on mathematics and the hard sciences. Most Platform Traders today have advances formal education and training in mathematics, probabilities, physics, computer science, economics, and engineering. Trade rooms are more similar to busy computer driven laboratories than the old image of guys in a boiler-room shouting into two telephones at one time. Almost all orders are input electronically and trades are matched up by sophisticated software. Private Placement Programmers and software engineers are indispensable to successful Private Placement Programs and Trade Platforms.

As mentioned earlier, Platform Traders have many products to trade and a huge number of global exchanges to execute the trades. The most well-known exchange in the world is the New York Stock Exchange (NYSE). When Platform Traders make a trade, that trade is executed on an exchange. The NYSE, CME, NYMEX, ICE, CBOE and NASDAQ are the largest U.S. exchanges. In Europe the LSE, Euronext and Frankfort Exchange are largest. In commodities much of the execution is done on the Globex, an electronic exchange. Platform Traders use the exchanges to buy and sell trillions of dollars of stocks, bonds, currencies, gold, oil, euro-dollars, CMO's, ETF's and hundreds of other securities, currencies, and derivatives in efforts to make profits for themselves and investors.

Private Placement Program Traders can make profits by buying a particular instrument or by shorting, (selling it) betting the price will go down. Some Platform Traders buy and sell similar instruments simultaneous, betting on the change in price between the two instruments; this is called arbitrage and spread trading. Other Platform Traders employ option strategies, such as writing options, writing straddles, strangles, butterflies and condors. Option strategies can quickly become extremely complex and are a highly specialized area of trading which requires extraordinary expertise.

Private Placement Trading Platforms utilize margin to buy and sell all of the various instruments they trade. Margin is simply a partial payment for the instrument. Most people are familiar with margin on stocks. Margins are met with cash, period. Contrary to what some people may believe, the only instrument that is good for backing a trade position is cash. When a profit is made, it is credited to the Trade Platforms books that day; when a loss is taken it is debited from the Trade Platforms books that day. Private Placement Platform Trading is a cash business; gains and losses are marked to market each day. Trade Platform Managers should know by between midnight and two a.m. each trading day where they stand. The Private Placement Trade Platforms maintain what is called a customer segregated account with an FCM. This account is where the Trade Platform Investors' funds are held. An independent capital account is established for each Trade Platform Investor in order to provide accurate accounting on a monthly or quarterly basis. The Private Placement Platforms' funds are deposited into a master segregated funds account to be used for margin in trading.

Goldman Sachs, Merrill Lynch, ABN AMRO, MF Global, JP Morgan Chase, Credit Suisse, Deutsche

Bank and Bank of America are all FCMs. These companies, as well as handling trades for independent Trade Platforms for many years, have had their own internal proprietary trading desk or Trade Platforms. Some of these trade desks are famous such as Goldman's Alpha Fund, Morgan Stanley's PDT (Process Driven Trading) Platform and Deutsche Bank's legendary SABA Trading Program, led by Boaz Weinstein. The new regulatory environment is forcing many of the banks to divest themselves of proprietary Trading Platforms. This is making for a large talent pool comprising the best and brightest traders available for Private Placement Programs, Private Hedge Funds and Trading Platforms.

Private Placement Programs and Trading Platforms often use what is known as notionalization or notional funding to increase the leverage that the Trade Platform may use. The Trading Platforms may leverage its trading capital as much as ten times, meaning that One Hundred Million Dollars ($100,000,000) may be traded as it was a Billion Dollars ($1,000,000,000). Leverage, while giving the ability to greatly increase the returns on cash can also lead to significant loss. The old adage that "leverage is a double-edge sword" is very true. Notionalization absolutely must be constantly monitored and adjusted, depending on margin requirements and market conditions. The Private Placement Platform Managers have investment committees that are responsible for determining notional trading levels. Notionalization is a very powerful tool for the Private Placement Trading Platforms.

Private Placement Program: The Process of PPP Trade

The private placement program / PPP trade is a money intensive program which requires high funding potentials. This program has been designed as a high investment trade where the profit margin is immense. The basic requirement to ply this trade is the ability to arrange for valid financial credits/asset valuation and risk management skills.

The application process:

Primarily a private investor is needed to complete the application process with appropriate documentation that validates his/her financial assets. Other paper documents include identity card, residential proofs, proofs for nationality and other essential information that qualifies a person as a living entity.

Importance of asset evaluation:

Amongst all the documents the asset evaluation plays an important part. It is based on this credential that an investor is granted or declined the proposal of private placement program or private trading. When considered for such a program the license issuing board pays considerable importance to the fact whether the assets are of floating or fixed origin. The fixed assets are the non-cash types, meaning that they cannot be adequately utilized while plying the private trade program. This may include types of personal bonds or other financial instruments that has been extended in an incorrect manner.

The verification part:

After the successful completion of the application process it now depends on the authorized board to meticulously speculate the financial strength of the client and judge whether he/she is capable of carrying out the requisites in a proper way. Verification of the submitted documents and their legitimacy also accounts for the sanction of the private trading license. In most cases it has been noted that the viable clients who are granted the opportunity of this profitable trade are the corporate houses. However, if private investors can suffice the required capital then their proposal may also stand the chance of being considered (subject to specifications).

One thing that is to be kept in mind while filing for application is that, the proposal for Private placement program license can be kept pending for weeks. The most suitable entrepreneur is given the first preference while others have to keep their patience and wait for their chance. Thus, the private placement program it can be concluded is not meant for every entrepreneur who wants to engage in lucrative business trade. Until and unless one gets a license for the concerned authority, he/she cannot take to the merchandise of PPP trade instruments.

Private Placement Offering

WHAT IS A "REG D" PRIVATE PLACEMENT OFFERING AND HOW CAN IT HELP RAISE CAPITAL FOR MY BUSINESS?

The Regulation D Offering is an exemption designed by the SEC for private business. It is the most widely used program the SEC offers and provides the proper exemption needed to raise capital from investors. Not raising capital properly can provide investors with a "right of rescission" in the future-meaning they have the right to have their investment returned to them regardless of the circumstances. You could also face fines and other penalties resulting from an improper sale of securities to investors.

HOW CAN I SOLICIT CAPITAL FROM INVESTORS?

A US or foreign company that is seeking to raise capital utilizing Regulation D exemption or any person acting on its behalf MAY NOT offer or sell its securities by any form of "general solicitation" or "general advertising." The use of mailing lists, unregulated referral sources (non-broker dealers), and other database providers can present problems to the company/issuer if they are not utilized and sourced properly.

To prevent the United States Securities and Exchange Commission ("SEC") from deeming your solicitation to be a general solicitation, the following conditions are required:

- There be a "pre-existing" relationship between the company/issuer and the prospective investor prior to the solicitation; and
- At the time an investment is made, the company/issuer has knowledge regarding the

sophistication or financial condition of the prospective investor

In order to fully comply with SEC Reg D rules, building your own investor database of "pre-existing" relationships with potential investors is the best way to raise capital and present your private placement offering to qualified investors.

Companies can also choose to utilize a Foreign Direct Stock Offering (Reg S) which would enable them to raise capital from foreign investors.

How Private Placement Programs / Trade Platforms Work

Many private placement programs and trade platforms are legitimate investment vehicles that are accessible to a wide variety of investors. An excellent white paper on private placement programs and trade platforms was written by MB Assets of Memphis, TN- a copy of which is available for download above. It should be noted that we have no relationship with MB Assets or its principals— their white paper is provided for educational purposes only and should not be construed as an endorsement of the firm.

Part of the confusion regarding private placement programs in particular is the term, "private placement". Private placements are used by companies to raise capital from private investors often via a set of investment documents known as a Private Placement Memorandum (PPM).

Prime Bank Programs

More often than not, when people refer to PPPs they are referring to what are more properly known as Prime Bank Programs. Prime Bank Programs, also known as Prime Bank Investments, High Yield Investment Programs (HYIPs), Buy-Sell Programs or Roll Programs, are clearly and universally fraudulent. They purport to involve the purchase and sale of medium-term notes (MTNs), Standby Letters of Credit (SBLCs), Bank Guarantees (BGs), or some similar instrument.

As the name implies, it is usually alleged that only the largest top-50 prime banks in the world are involved in this program and participation is by invitation only. There is usually a great deal of secrecy involved and the minimum investment is typically in excess of $100 million or more. Interestingly enough, prime bank programs in the US often state that only overseas banks are involved while overseas programs often state that only US banks are involved.

They are most often described as "risk-free" investments where one prime bank issues discounted instruments to a purchaser at another prime bank who has committed to purchase the notes at an agreed-upon price. If this is simply a bank-to-bank transaction one might wonder where the scam comes in. Supposedly, the purchasing bank needs a large deposit from a new client to create the line of credit that will be used for the purchase. This deposit will be placed in a "blocked" account and held untouched by the bank until the transaction has been completed.

Prime bank programs have been universally condemned by the FBI, SEC and US Treasury Department as being fraudulent. In recent years, fraudsters have attempted to circumvent these governmental warnings with a clever ruse. They state that these agencies know that the programs are real, but that they are obligated to publicly deny their existence lest investors transfer large amounts of capital from deposit accounts into prime bank programs. Supposedly, this mass exodus of capital would cause the banking system to collapse, hence the official denials. This, of course, is complete nonsense.

Medium Term Notes (MTNs), Standby Letters of Credit (SBLCs) and Bank Guarantees (BGs)

Part of the reasons such frauds have been successful is that Medium Term Notes, Bank Guarantees and Standby Letters of Credit are real financial instruments. A Medium-Term Note is the general name given to a debt instrument that matures in the medium term, typically 5-10 years. Bank Guarantees, as they are known outside of the US, or their US counterpart, Standby Letters of Credit, are most often used in international commerce where a seller might be unsure about a buyer's ability to pay for goods once received. One way of overcoming this impasse is to utilize a bank guarantee or standby letter of credit.

A SBLC or BG is simply a promise to pay on the part of the bank involved in the transaction. Trading partners often have greater confidence in a transaction if the payment is backed by a commercial bank rather than a trading partner with whom they might be unfamiliar. Banks are not in the business of losing depositors' money, so in order for them to issue a SBLC or BG in the first place, they would underwrite the SBLC/BG similar to an unsecured loan-meaning obtaining an SBLC/BG is a difficult endeavor to begin with.

Moreover, banks will often charge 1%-8% of the face value of the instrument, meaning a $100 million SBLC could cost the bank's client as much as $8 million to obtain, and is usually only valid for a period of one year. Which, of course, begs the question: if the borrower has sufficient standing with the bank to be approved for an SBLC/BG and sufficient funds to cover the cost of issuing it, why are they contacting us? The answer is, if this were a legitimate transaction, they wouldn't be.

Over the years many people have approached us looking for SBLCs/BGs. Most are actually looking to LEASE an SBLC/BG and use the instrument as collateral for a loan or cash investment. This is somewhat akin to leasing a new car and then trying to use the car as collateral for a loan from another lender. No automobile, SBLC, BG or any other leased asset can be used as collateral in a legitimate financial transaction, which is why these transactions never work.

Issuing in the private placement market offers companies a variety of advantages, including maintaining confidentiality, accessing long-term, fixed- rate capital, diversifying financing sources and creating additional financing capacity.

One of the most common questions we hear from CEOs and CFOs is, "Why would I issue a private placement?" A private placement is a method for both public and private companies to raise capital through the private sale of corporate debt or equity securities, to a limited number of qualified investors (aka lenders); it is an alternative to traditional capital sources, such as bank debt, or issuing securities on the public bond market.

Differences Between Private Placement Program and Public Offering

The securities are sold to a group of investors in the private placement of shares whereas in public offering the securities are offered to the public.

Private placement of shares can be issued by both public and private Companies whereas in case of public offering the Company is either listed or will be listed after the offer is made.

This placement deals may not be required to be registered with a regulator whereas the deals in which securities are offered publicly have to be registered with a regulator.

How Does Private Placement Program Affect the Share Price of a Company?

The private placement of shares, if done by a private company will not affect the share price because they are not listed. However, for a public listed Company, this placement will lead to a decline in share price at least in the near term.

This placement leads to dilution of the ownership of the existing shareholders to a proportion of the size of this placement. This is because new shares are issued and the holdings of the existing shareholders remain the same. Let us see an example:

Let the number of shares outstanding before the private placement of shares by 10 million and the Company has proposed to offer 1 million equity shares in the private placement Thus, this would result in dilution of ownership of the existing shareholders by 10%.

This dilution of a share normally leads to the decline of the share price; the impact of this placement can be considered as similar to that of a stock split. However, such an impact can be seen only in the short-term, a long-term effect on the price would take into account the utilization of funds by the Company raised during this placement If the Company does a private placement of shares to raise capital for a project which could provide better returns; extra profits and revenue from such a project will impact the share price thus pushing it higher.

Restrictions Affecting Private Placement

The SEC formerly placed many restrictions on private placement transactions. For example, such offerings could only be made to a limited number of investors, and the company was required to establish strict criteria for each investor to meet. Furthermore, the SEC required private placement of securities to be made only to "sophisticated" investors—those capable of evaluating the merits and understanding the risks associated with the investment. Finally, stock sold through private offerings could not be advertised to the public and could only be resold under certain circumstances.

In 1992, however, the SEC eliminated many of these restrictions in order to make it easier for small companies to raise capital through private placements of securities. The rules now allow companies to promote their private placement offerings more broadly and to sell the stock to a greater number of buyers. It is also easier for investors to resell such securities. Although the SEC restrictions on private placements were relaxed, it is nonetheless important for small business owners to understand the various federal and state laws affecting such transactions and to take the appropriate procedural steps. It may be helpful to assemble a team of qualified legal and accounting professionals before attempting to undertake a private placement.

Many of the rules affecting private placements are covered under Section 4(2) of the federal securities law. This section provides an exemption for companies wishing to sell up to $5million in securities to a small number of accredited investors. Companies conducting an offering under Section 4(2) cannot solicit investors publicly, and the majority of investors are expected to be either insiders (company management) or sophisticated outsiders with a preexisting relationship with the company (professionals, suppliers, customers, etc.). At a minimum, the companies are expected to provide potential investors with recent financial statements, a list of risk factors associated with the investment, and an invitation to inspect their facilities. In most respects, the preparation and disclosure requirements for offerings under Section 4(2) are similar to Regulation D filings.

Regulation D—which was adopted in 1982 and has been revised several times since—consists of a set of rules numbered 501 through 508. Rules 504, 505, and 506 describe three different types of exempt offerings and set forth guidelines covering the amount of stock that can be sold and the number and type of investors that are allowed under each one. Rule 504 covers the Small Corporate Offering Registration, or SCOR. SCOR gives an exemption to private companies that raise no more than $1 million in any 12-month period through the sale of stock. There are no restrictions on the number or types of investors, and the stock may be freely traded. The SCOR process is easy enough for a small business owner to complete with the assistance of a knowledgeable accountant and attorney. It is available in all states except Delaware, Florida, Hawaii, and Nebraska.

Rule 505 enables a small business to sell up to $5 million in stock during a 12-month period to an unlimited number of investors, provided that no more than 35 of them are non-accredited. To be accredited, an investor must have sufficient assets or income to make such an investment According to the SEC rules, individual investors must have either $1 million in assets (other than their home and car) or $200,000 in net annual personal income, while institutions must hold $million in assets. Finally, Rule 506 allows a company to sell unlimited securities to an unlimited number of investors, provided that no more than 35 of them are non-accredited. Under Rule 506, investors must be sophisticated. In both of these options, the securities cannot be freely traded.

Private Placement Program Advantages

One major advantage of private placement is that the issuer isn't subject to the SEC's strict regulations for a typical public offering. With a private placement, the issuing company isn't subject to the same disclosure and reporting requirements as a publicly offered bond.

Furthermore, privately placed bonds don't require credit-agency ratings. Private placement is the cost and time-related savings involved. Issuing bonds publicly means incurring significant underwriter fees, while issuing them privately can save money.

Similarly, the process can be expedited when done in a private manner. Furthermore, private placement deals can be custom-built to meet the financial needs of both the issuer and investors.

- The biggest advantage with respect to private placements is the fact that most regulations governing public offerings do not come into play. Transactions are smoothers and a lot of crucial time is saved by not having to register through the Stock Exchange.
- The acquiring of necessary capital becomes a much speedier process. It also becomes safer for the start up or company in question, since such acquisitions can be risky in the early growing stages of any enterprise.
- Investors have a good opportunity to negotiate and reduce the cost of the securities to a price they can afford and that is lucrative for their personal business.
- Long term and complex financings of lesser known companies can be made possible through this. It also allows a company flexibility in terms of choosing their own investors and remaining a private company.

Other Advantages

Long Term Advantage - If it is a debt security, the Company issues private placement bonds which generally have a longer time to mature than a bank liability. Thus, the Company will have more time to pay back the investors. This is ideal for the situations where the Company is investing in new businesses that would require time to earn and grow. Further, if this placement is done on equity shares; they are generally done to strategic investors with a "buy-and-hold" strategy. These investors invest for a longer duration and also provide strategic inputs on running the business. Thus, the Company benefits from having a long-time relationship with the investor.

Less Execution timeframe - As the market for this placement has matured this has increased standardization of documentation, better terms, and pricing and increased the size of raising funds. Further, the issuer does not have to register and market such a fundraising exercise with the regulator, hence it can be executed in lesser time and cost. If the issuer is issuing private placement bonds that will be privately held, he may not be required to get credit rating which will further reduce the cost to be paid to the credit agency.

Diversification of Fundraising - Fundraising by this placement helps the Company to diversify Company's funding sources and its capital structure. It aids the Company in raising capital when market liquidity conditions are not good. It helps the Company to organize the capital structure in terms of debt-equity structure and help it to manage its debt obligations.

Lesser Regulatory Requirements - This placement requires limited public disclosures and is prone to less regulatory requirements than that would be needed in a public offering. Thus, the Company would negotiate the deal privately and offer the securities at a negotiated and fixed price.

Sell to Accredited Investors - This placement issuer can sell complex securities to the investors participating in the issue because such an issue will be limited to a select group of investors (accredited investors). Further, they would understand the potential risk and return on such securities.

Private Placement Program Disadvantages

One major disadvantage of private placement is that bond issuers will frequently have to pay higher interest rates to entice investors. Because privately placed bonds aren't assigned ratings, it can be trickier for investors to determine their risk. Issuers must therefore be prepared to pay investors a premium in exchange for taking on added risk.

In addition, private placement limits the number and variety of investors the issuing party can reach, so selling bonds privately could be more challenging than doing so publicly. In some situations, private placement may cause an issuer to spend more time and money finding and attracting investors than a public offering would require, thus negating one of the primary benefits of avoiding a public listing.

Finally, private-placement issuers could be forced to take extra steps to cater to their investors. For example, potential investors might demand additional equity from issuers or impose other such stipulations in exchange for their investment dollars.

Even if a company chooses to sell its bonds privately, it must still comply with certain SEC rules for private placement These rules apply to aspects such as the number and monetary value of bonds being offered and the methods used to advertise them.

- Agreements may not always be clearly spelt out due to the lack of a detailed prospectus, and one's expectations of performance may not be realized.
- The shares and bonds are always required to be placed at a discounted price in order to offer incentives for investment. This increases risks for loss.

Other Advantages

Difficulty in Finding a suitable investor - First and foremost, the disadvantage of a private placement of shares would be to find a suitable investor. Further, the investor may have a limited amount of funds to invest and may set certain targets to be achieved whereby he would invest the funds.

Higher Returns Requirement - The investors may require more return because of the risk they are taking by investing privately. If the investment is for private placement bonds, they may ask for higher interest rates or annual coupons because of the risk they take for unrated bond securities and illiquid securities. If investment in a private Company is by an issue of equity shares, they may ask for higher equity ownership or board positions because of the liquidity risk of their investment. Further, even if the Company is publicly traded and it chooses to offer private placement shares, the investors would do a due diligence and some clauses on such an offer like annual dividends or shares to be issued at cheaper than market rates as they would have to lock-in their stake (not to be sold in open market) for a certain time period.

CHAPTER 2

Private Placement Invest Debt Contracts Terms

Private placements generally have fixed interest rates, intermediate-to long-term maturities, and moderately large issue sizes. Their contracts frequently include restrictive covenants. These terms differ from those found in other markets for debt, for example, the markets for bank loans and publicly issued bonds.

Issue Size

On average, private placements are larger than bank loans and smaller than public bonds. In 1989, the median new commercial and industrial (C&I) bank loan was for about $50,000; more than 96 percent were less than $10 million. When loan size distributions were computed by volume rather than number, large loans naturally accounted for a larger share. The mean loan size was about $1 million. The 3.6 percent of loans for $10 million or more accounted for 58 percent of total loan volume. Although most are small, loans for as much as $100 million are not extraordinary.

In contrast, the median private placement issued by nonfinancial corporations in 1989 was $32 million, and the mean was $76 million. None was less than $250,000 (compared with 70 percent of bank loans in that category). Most private placements were for amounts between $10 million and $100 million.

The median public issue was $150 million, and the mean public issue was $181 million. Most public issues were larger than $100 million. None was smaller than $10 million, and only 15 percent were smaller than $100 million.

In interviews, market participants often remarked that the private market is cost-effective mainly for issues larger than $10 million, whereas the public market is cost-effective for issues larger than $100 million. The data are consistent with this assertion, as only 10 percent to 15 percent of private placements and underwritten public issues (excluding medium-term note issues) fall below the respective boundaries.

These cross-market patterns in size of financing are often attributed to economies of scale in issue size, that is, to declining costs to the issuer, including fees and interest costs, as issue size increases. Such arguments are usually based on a perception that, holding all else constant, interest rates are lowest in the public market and highest in the bank loan market and on a perception that fixed costs of issuance are highest in the public market, smaller in the private market, and lowest in the bank loan market.

An alternative, possibly overlapping explanation is that the three markets specialize in providing different kinds of financing to different kinds of borrowers and that relevant borrower characteristics are associated with issue size. In particular, borrowers of large amounts are often big and well-established firms that require relatively little initial due diligence and loan monitoring by lenders, whereas those borrowing small amounts often require much due diligence and monitoring. Thus, borrowers of small-to-moderate amounts usually must borrow in the private placement or bank loan markets, where lenders are organized to serve information- problematic borrowers, whereas those borrowing larger amounts usually can issue in the public market because they are not information problematic. Both explanations are important, but the second explanation is probably more important in determining the market in which a borrower issues debt.

Prepayment Penalties and Maturity

According to their maturity distributions, commercial and industrial bank loans tend to have relatively short maturities, private placements tend to have intermediate-to long-term maturities, and public bonds have the highest proportion of long maturities. In 1989, the median bank loan had a maturity of just over three months, and the mean maturity was around nine months. Almost 80 percent of loans had maturities of less than one year. When weighted by loan size, two- thirds of loans had maturities shorter than one month. In interviews, market participants often stated that banks seldom lend long term, even when the loan interest rate floats. They stated that loans in the three-to five-year range are not uncommon, five- to seven-year loans are less common, and loans longer than seven years are rare. These remarks are supported by the charts.

The distributions in the charts are for a non-random sample of new loans, not for loans on the books. Because very short-term loans stay on the books for only a short time, a maturity distribution for a bank's portfolio of loans at a specific time would be less skewed toward the short end. Such a distribution, however, would probably still show banks to have relatively few loans with maturities longer than seven years.

Private placements are generally intermediate to long term. The median nonfinancial private placement had a maturity of nine years, and the mean maturity was also about nine years. No private placements had maturities shorter than one year. A moderate fraction had intermediate maturities, but about two-thirds had maturities of seven years or longer. The median average life of private placements is between six and seven years; many private placements include sinking fund provisions that cause their average lives to be significantly

Distribution of average lives of fixed-rate private placement commitments measured as a percentage of the total value of new private commitments by major life insurance companies, January 1990-July 1992 Percent

The median maturity of our sample of bonds issued in 1989 was ten years, and the mean maturity almost thirteen years. Only 17 percent had a maturity of less than seven years. The median average life of public bonds was around ten years.

From the standpoint of financial theory, this cross¬market pattern of maturity distributions is a bit of a puzzle. Even if long-term borrowers have a strong preference for fixed rates, banks could in principle make long-term, fixed-rate loans and execute swaps to obtain payment streams matching their floating rate liabilities. Apparently, however, they seldom do so. One explanation may be that the cost of swaps and other hedges is sufficient to make such loans unattractive to banks. Another possibility is that the different markets tend to serve borrowers that require different amounts of credit evaluation and monitoring and that in equilibrium such differences are responsible for cross¬market patterns in many contract terms, including maturities.

Privately placed debt contracts almost always include strong call protection in the form of punitive prepayment penalties. Buyers of private placements usually fund their purchases with long-term, fixed-rate liabilities, and call protection is an important part of their strategy for controlling interest rate risk. Prepayment penalties in the private market generally require the issuer to pay the present value of the remaining payment stream (principal plus interest at the contracted rate) at a discount rate equal to the Treasury rate plus some spread, frequently 50 basis points, but sometimes even zero. The discount rate for a nonpunitive call-protection provision includes a risk premium similar to that of the security itself (that is, associated with the credit quality of the security). When the discount rate fails to include a sufficiently high premium, the lender realizes an economic gain if the security is prepaid, even if the security is matched with liabilities of equal duration.

In the past decade, publicly issued bonds have included increasing call protection. Crabbe (1991) presents statistics indicating that 78 percent of public bonds issued in 1990 were noncallable for life, whereas only 5 percent of those issued in 1980 were noncallable. Bank loans are typically prepayable at any time at par.

Types of Payment Yields and Stream

Most bank loans carry floating interest rates, whereas most private and public bond issues carry fixed rates. Only 3 percent of commitments by major life insurance companies to purchase private placements from January 1990 to July 1992 carried floating rates. Only 95 of the 1,588 private placements of debt recorded in the Investment Dealers' Digest (IDD) database for 1989 are listed as having floating rates.

The 95 represented 6 percent of issues and accounted for 14.3 percent of volume. However, many of the floating-rate financings in the IDD sample may, in effect, have been bank loans, so the latter statistics probably substantially overstate the fraction of private placements with floating rates. About 5 percent of the volume of public bonds issued in 1989 had variable rates.

Publicly available data on private placement yields in recent years are limited. However, many market participants stated that the yield spreads over Treasuries on traditional investment- grade private placements are higher than the spreads for publicly issued bonds with similar credit risk. The average differential between private and public spreads varies over time, but participants spoke of a range of 10 to 40 basis points. The differential is often called a liquidity premium, but it must also compensate lenders for any costs of credit evaluation and monitoring. The term credit analysis premium might be more appropriate.

Some market participants noted that spreads on investment-grade private placements are occasionally lower than those on comparable publics for very brief periods, up to a few days. They attributed this difference to slower adjustment of the private market to changes in the yield curve.

Spreads on below-investment-grade private placements have often been below those on comparable public junk bonds. Investors may demand larger risk premiums on public junk bonds because employing the risk control technologies of lender due diligence and loan monitoring is more difficult in the public markets or because comparatively rated public issues actually are riskier.

Several researchers have examined the relation between issuer quality and yield spread in alternative markets by focusing on the difference between the private placement and the public bond markets. For the 1951¬61 period, Cohan (1967) found that the spread between yields on private placements and yields on public bonds rose as the credit quality of the issuer increased. Thus, the private placement market was relatively more attractive for lower quality credits. In a study that controlled for the restrictiveness of covenants, Hawkins (1982) confirmed this result for the period 1975-77. These results are consistent with our discussions with market participants, who indicated that the public market tended to have relatively little appetite for small¬sized, low- quality issues. However, this statement does not necessarily hold for larger-sized, low-quality securities. The development of the junk bond market in the 1980s produced a competitive public market for large, non-investment-grade bonds.

Thus, Cohan's and Hawkins's findings may not hold for larger issues in the second half of the 1980s. Moreover, the credit crunch in the below- investment-grade sector of the private placement market since mid-1990 has led to a significant increase in the average spreads for below- investment-grade private placements of all sizes.

Variety of Securities

A wide variety of securities, including secured, unsecured, asset-backed, senior, and subordinated, is issued in the private placement market. The different types appearing in the IDD database for 1989, with the number of issues and the volume for each type.

Covenants

Loans to information-problematic borrowers, which are typically medium-sized or smaller borrowers, generally have tighter covenants than loans to less-information- problematic borrowers. Covenants are one mechanism that lenders can use to reduce the likelihood of borrowers' taking actions that might lead to an expropriation of wealth from lenders. In the absence of covenant restrictions, smaller borrowers are, on average, more likely to attempt such expropriations. They often have less to lose in terms of reputation and are typically more information-problematic so that detection and control of expropriation attempts are more difficult for lenders.

Thus, the more information problematic the borrower, the larger the number and the tighter the nature of covenants by lenders. Stated differently, lenders offer smaller, more problematic borrowers lower interest rates in return for tighter covenants, and thus such borrowers are more willing to negotiate debt contracts that include tight covenants. Moreover, without such covenants, lenders might refuse to make loans to such borrowers regardless of the interest rate.

Covenants in any debt contract are either affirmative covenants, negative covenants, or financial covenants (which are a subset of negative covenants). Affirmative covenants require a borrower to meet certain standards of behavior.

They include requirements that the firm stay in the same business and meet its legal and contractual obligations. They are common in public bonds, private placements, and bank loans. Negative covenants restrain the borrowing firm from taking actions that would be detrimental to the bondholders. They include restrictions on capital expenditures, on the sale of assets, on dividends and other payments, on the types of investments that the firm can make, on the amount of additional debt that the firm can incur, on liens that the firm can give to other lenders, and on merger and acquisition activity.

Financial covenants restrict measurable financial variables and can stipulate, for example, mini- mums to be maintained on capital, the ratio of assets to liabilities, working capital, current ratio (current assets/current liabilities), or the ratio of earnings to fixed charges. A financial covenant can be either a maintenance covenant or an incurrence covenant. With a maintenance covenant, the criterion set forth in the covenant must be met on a regular basis, say at the end of each quarter. With an incurrence covenant, the criterion must be met at the time of a prespecified event, such as the firm's making an acquisition or incurring additional debt.

The number and the tightness of negative and especially financial covenants in private placements are associated with the quality of the issuer, that is, with the degree of both its information problems and its observable risk. Tightness refers to the likelihood that a particular covenant will be binding in the future. Private placements for lower-quality issuers often include many financial covenants. Contracts for moderately risky issuers often include only one or two financial covenants with minimum values farther from current values and thus less likely to be violated. Highly rated issues (A or better) usually have no financial covenants, unless their average life exceeds seven years, in which case an incurrence covenant on a debt ratio is often included. Most financial covenants in private placements are incurrence covenants, although occasionally one or two maintenance covenants may be included, especially when these are designed to match maintenance covenants in other debt of the issuer, such as bank loans.

Bank loan agreements typically contain only maintenance covenants. Financial covenants in bank loan agreements are reportedly generally tighter than in private placements, even for borrowers with the same characteristics. As with private placements, the number and the tightness of bank loan financial covenants depend on the quality of the issuer. Loans to small and medium- sized borrowers typically include many financial covenants. Very large companies, however, generally obtain bank loan facilities, frequently in the form of unfunded loan commitments, without meaningful financial covenants.

Indentures in publicly traded bonds, even for below-investment-grade bonds, generally contain no financial covenants. Beginning in 1992, however, some public junk bonds included financial covenants, especially debt ratio and interest coverage covenants. Market participants disagree on whether this development is permanent or transitory. Some participants assert that such issues were bought by investors that did not fully understand the nature of the monitoring and renegotiation activities associated with their purchases and that these investors will stop buying such issues at some future time. Others assert that such issues are, in effect, illiquid and were bought by mutual funds with staffs of credit analysts, making the instruments functionally equivalent to below-investment-grade private placements. This difference of opinion may not be resolved until some of the securities deteriorate in quality and must be renegotiated.

Covenants and Renegotiation

Covenants can limit a borrowing firm's flexibility in financial and strategic policymaking. The constraint on flexibility can, however, be relaxed through implicit or explicit provisions for contract renegotiation, thus increasing borrowers' willing-ness to accept tight covenants. For example, if the pursuit of a new strategy, such as the acquisition of another firm, would violate an existing covenant, the borrower may request that the debt contract be renegotiated. It might, for example, request a waiver of the covenant. The lender analyzes the effect of the new strategy, and if the lender can establish that it will improve the prospects of the firm without increasing the risk to the lender, the lender may agree to waive or adjust the covenant Even if the new strategy increases the risk of the loan as it is presently structured, the lender may grant a waiver if the borrowing firm agrees to adjust other terms of the debt contract. In effect, banks, insurance companies, and other lenders to information-problematic borrowers offer contracts that limit borrower incentives to take risks and still permit flexibility through contract renegotiation. They can offer flexible contracts because of their ability to monitor and analyze borrowers.

One reason information-problematic firms seldom borrow in the public market is that the benefits of covenants are hard to capture there because diffuse ownership makes them difficult to renegotiate. Knowing that renegotiation with many lenders is very costly, public bond issuers are willing to include at most a few loose covenants. Because many covenants are not feasible in public debt, much of the monitoring technology of information-intensive lenders is not useful for public debt, as public bond buyers may have no legal mechanism for controlling excessively risky borrower behavior even if they detect it.

Thus, many information-problematic firms are unable to borrow in the public market.

This discussion implies that bank loans, private placements, and public bonds will differ not only in the number and the tightness of covenants, but also in the frequency with which the covenants are renegotiated. As noted, the covenants in bank loans are often relatively tight, implying a high frequency of renegotiation because bank borrowers. Those covenants that do appear in publicly issued bonds are relatively loose, implying a low frequency of covenant renegotiation. Private placement covenants and renegotiation rates fall between the two extremes but are generally closer to those of bank loans. The covenants in a private placement are typically violated several times during the life of the security, requiring several waivers or other renegotiations of terms

Including extensive, customized covenants is possible in private placements and commercial loans partly because both are negotiated debt instruments. Issuers and lenders can tailor contract terms in a way that satisfies the objectives of both as much as possible. Publicly issued bonds, which are underwritten without any direct negotiation between the issuer and the investors, are seldom customized.

Collateral

Some private placements are asset-backed securities, such as leveraged leases, collateralized trust certificates, and collateralized mortgage obligations. Also, a significant fraction of traditional private placements of straight and subordinated debt, such as first and second mortgage bonds, are secured.

Approximately one-third of the private placements in Kwan and Carleton's sample were secured. Similarly, 6 percent of the volume of private issues in 1989 was asset-backed, and 21 percent was otherwise secured, for a total of 27 percent secured. Asset-backed securities are more common in the public market, whereas collateral is much less common in other forms of public debt. In 1989, 24 percent of public issuance was asset-backed, and only 4 percent was otherwise secured. A much larger fraction of bank loans is secured. Statistics from the Federal Reserve's Survey of Terms of Bank Lending and the Federal Reserve/Small Business Administration's National Survey of Small Business Finance indicate that about two-thirds of commercial bank loans to nonfinancial businesses are secured.

Conventional wisdom suggests that bank loans frequently involve collateral because bank borrowers are relatively risky; collateral is less often used in the private placement market because private placements tend to be less risky on average than bank loans; and collateral is infrequently used in the public debt market because of the high quality of the average issuer. collateral is useful not only for controlling observable risks but also for solving information problems. Collateral in debt contracts helps minimize the incentives of firm owners to act in ways that are detrimental to lenders.

Because these incentives are more acute in smaller, more information-problematic firms, collateral is widespread in the bank loan market but rare in the public bond market.

Bank Loans

Bank loans typically have floating rates and short- to intermediate-term maturities and are relatively small and prepayable at par. They tend to include relatively tight financial covenants and thus must frequently be renegotiated. Private placements typically have fixed rates and intermediate- to long-term maturities, are moderately large, and include punitive prepayment penalties. Many include financial covenants.

Though these covenants are usually looser than those in bank loans, and thus are less easily violated, a typical private placement is renegotiated at some point. A significant number of private placements include no financial covenants, and thus renegotiation is less frequent for them.

Publicly issued bonds are typically fixed-rate, long-term, large loans. The presence of prepayment penalties and other call protection has varied over time. They seldom include financial covenants and are seldom renegotiated.

Individual lenders and borrowers take this cross-market pattern of terms as given and choose the market(s) with preferable terms. The next section explains why borrowers choose the private placement market, and section 4 explains why lenders do so.

Private Placement Market Borrowers

Borrowers in the private placement market generally fall into one or more categories. Most are information-problematic firms or, if they are not, their financings are complex enough that only information-intensive lenders will be willing to buy them. Others have specialized needs that are a disincentive to public issuance, such as a desire to avoid the disclosure associated with registration. Finally, some have issues too small to be done cost-effectively in the public market.

Firms that are not information problematic and that want to issue nonproblematic securities in large amounts generally borrow in the public markets. Those wishing to borrow for short terms or at floating rates generally borrow from banks (or similar intermediaries, like finance companies) or issue commercial paper. Some firms with a preference for long-term and fixed- rate funds, other things equal, may nevertheless end up borrowing for short terms and at floating rates from banks.

In describing U.S. capital markets, market participants often speak of a hierarchy of borrowers and debt markets based on a concept of borrower access. In this hierarchy, nonproblematic firms with nonproblematic issues can borrow in any market; and, for any given financing, they choose the market offering the best terms.

Information-problematic firms or issues, however, effectively have no access to the public markets, because public market lenders are not prepared to perform the necessary due diligence and monitoring. Moderately problematic firms may borrow in either the bank or the private placement market, whereas very information- problematic firms must use the bank loan market or cannot issue any outside debt (that is, they may be able to borrow only from those with ownership interest).

From a broad economic perspective, this hierarchy and the differential access of borrowers are not exogenous restrictions on borrowers' actions but are features of an economic equilibrium that is the outcome of choices by both borrowers and lenders. For example, in principle information-problematic borrowers could issue securities publicly, and public bond market lenders could acquire the expertise needed to perform due diligence and loan monitoring. In reality, however, the choices of lenders and borrowers have resulted in an equilibrium in which information- problematic firms and financings rarely appear in the public markets (for an analysis of the economic forces resulting in this equilibrium). In this section, we employ the concepts of access and of a hierarchy of borrowers because they are practical and simplify exposition when the focus is on borrowers alone, taking lenders and the broad market structure as given. We emphasize, however, that the current pattern of access is not set in stone but could change if the economic fundamentals changed.

The set of firms with access to the private market but not to the public market is not the same as the set of private market borrowers. Some private issues are by companies that have access to the public market but choose the private market for special reasons. Similarly, by asserting that very information-problematic firms typically must borrow from banks, we do not mean to imply that all bank borrowers are problematic. In fact, banks serve a wide variety of borrowers.

In the remainder of this section, we explain the taxonomy in more detail and then present supporting empirical evidence. The evidence suggests that, as a group, firms with access only to the bank loan and private placement markets differ in several respects from those that have access to the public bond market. Most notably, the average borrower in the former group is significantly smaller than the average issuer in the public bond market. Smaller-sized issuers are often more information problematic and thus must borrow in an information-intensive market.

Similarly, firms with access only to the bank loan market are significantly smaller and more information problematic than those having access to the private placement market. Another difference is that the private placements of companies issuing in both the public and the private markets tend to be considerably larger and more complex than private placements issued by companies that borrow only in the private market.

Our principal explanation for these facts involves economic theories centered on asymmetric information, but at least two other explanations are possible. One is that small firms tend to issue in small amounts and differential fixed costs of issuance make the net cost of obtaining funds for relatively small issues lower in the private market. Another possibility is that smaller firms tend to have higher observable risk and different classes of lending institution may have different incentives to take risks.

Mispriced deposit insurance may give banks the largest incentives to take risks, whereas the absence of any guarantees may give public bond buyers the smallest. State guaranty associations for life insurance companies, which offer policyholders some protection if their insurer fails, provide intermediate incentives.

The three explanations of market choice are not necessarily mutually exclusive. The evidence offers most support for the explanation centered on differences in information problems across firms, some support for differential fixed costs of issuance as a decisive factor in some cases, and little support for the explanation centered on differences in observable risk across firms. The two most important weaknesses of the third explanation are that contract terms (especially covenants) are systematically different in the public and private markets for firms with the same bond rating and that enlarging the set of lending institutions under consideration reveals inconsistencies. Finance companies, for example, enjoy no guarantees similar to deposit insurance and yet reportedly lend mainly to high-risk borrowers. All of the evidence is consistent with the view that the private market normally receives issues that require lender due diligence or loan monitoring. Our characterization of and explanation for the hierarchy thus focuses on differences in information problems.

Private Placement Market Issuers

Most private placements carry fixed interest rates and are of intermediate- to long-term maturity. Because firms generally find short-term and floating- rate loans no harder to obtain than long-term, fixed-rate loans, we infer that private issuers prefer a fixed rate and a long term. 41 In this study, we do not analyze firms' reasons for seeking long-term, fixed-rate debt financing. Commonly cited motivations include a desire to reduce the uncertainty associated with interest rate fluctuations or with funding long-term investments with short-term loans.

Broad Industry Types of Issuers

Most issuers of private placements are nonfinancial businesses or financial institutions. In 1989, businesses accounted for 61 percent of the total volume of private placements and financial institutions for 30 percent. State and local governments were responsible for only thirty-one issues in 1989, and only four were for more than $25 million.

Information-problematic Firms

Borrowers that are information problematic have access to the bank loan market for working capital and intermediate-term loans, but normally they cannot obtain longer-term financing in the public bond market, as buyers of publicly offered bonds generally do not devote staff and other resources to the credit analysis required for investment in these companies. Investors in private placements, however, have developed the necessary capacity for initial due diligence and loan monitoring and have achieved economies of scale enabling them to offer favorable borrowing terms to information- problematic firms.

The information problems that borrowers pose for lenders span a spectrum. A firm's position on this spectrum tends to be correlated with both its size and its observable credit risk. Information problems posed for lenders tend to increase as borrower size decreases partly because smaller firms enter into fewer externally visible contracts with employees, customers, and suppliers. Larger firms enter into more contracts and larger dollar volumes of contracts. The terms of these contracts, and the large firms' performance under them, are generally observable at relatively low cost; for example, they are often reported in the financial press. Facts about contract performance reveal information about a firm's likely future performance, and when such facts are widely available, a firm will find building a reputation for good performance easier. In general, the larger the costs to a firm of losing its good reputation, the smaller the agency problems that must be managed by its lenders.

Size may also be related to information problems because size is correlated with age. Younger firms, which tend to be smaller, generally have not yet had time to acquire a reputation. Similarly, observable credit risk may be positively correlated with information problems because risk is correlated with age. Younger firms tend to be riskier because they may not yet have achieved organizational stability and the marketability of their product lines may not be well established. Risk may also be associated with information problems because the incentive to engage in behavior that expropriates wealth from lenders is more acute in observably riskier firms.

Most issuers of private placements are medium- sized firms and can be described as only moderately problematic. Very problematic, typically small borrowers usually lack access to the private market, where lenders' capacity for due diligence and especially for monitoring is often not as high as that of banks and some other lenders. Such borrowers may also be able to obtain better terms in the bank market. A bank loan generally contains more restrictive covenants than a private placement, has a considerably shorter maturity, and involves more monitoring by the bank.

Consequently, smaller companies borrowing from banks are, in effect, issuing a safer security than they would have issued in the private placement market and can thus obtain a lower rate. 46 The shorter maturities, tighter covenants, and floating rates may make bank loans less-than-perfect substitutes for private placements for such companies, but such terms may be preferable to no loan at all or to a loan with a very high interest rate.

Extremely problematic borrowers, such as start-up or very small firms, may be unable to issue outside debt, especially straight debt, and may be forced to rely on equity financing. Sources of long-term funding for such companies include equity funds, mezzanine debt funds, and venture capital funds. These sources are particularly attractive to firms that are unable to provide collateral for an intermediate-term bank loan. Equity and mezzanine debt funds typically extend financing through a combination of subordinated debt and equity. The principal difference between the two is that equity funds usually require a larger equity interest—often in excess of 20-25 percent. Venture capital funds typically invest in developing companies and require an equity interest. Again, these alternative sources, like bank loans, are not perfect substitutes for standard private placements, as they require the borrower to give up an equity interest in the firm. For many smaller, owner- managed firms, this may be a drawback. However, equity funds may be the only source of financing for those firms too small or too risky even for the bank loan market.

Firms with Information-problematic Financings

Large, non-information-problematic firms with complex financing requirements have often used the private placement market. Such companies tend to issue straight debt in the public bond market but turn to the private placement market for complex transactions that public market investors are not well prepared to evaluate. Private placement investors have developed the specialized skills for analyzing the credit risk of these transactions and can command loan spreads sufficient to provide a satisfactory return on their services. Examples of such transactions are project financings, capitalized equipment leases, joint ventures, and new types of asset- backed securities. The private placement market often serves as a testing ground for new types of securities, which may eventually move to the public market as investors become more familiar with their structure and the methods for analyzing their credit risk. One frequently cited example is asset-backed securities, which reportedly originated in the private market but are now issued in the public market as well.

Firms with Specialized Needs

Another category of firms using the private placement market consists of borrowers that could issue in the public bond market—and in some instances have done so—but turn to the private market for reasons unrelated to the complexity of their financings. Included in this group are privately held U.S. companies and foreign companies that wish to preserve their privacy. Foreign issuers in the U.S. private placement market also avoid the conformance to U.S. generally accepted accounting principles that would be required if they issued in the public debt market. Corporations contemplating acquisitions or takeovers also have often relied upon the private placement market to protect the confidentiality of their transactions and thus decrease the likelihood of competing offers.

Many large companies have used the private placement market to raise funds when time is a factor. For example, when in 1989 the Congress significantly curtailed the tax advantages of issuing debt for Employee Stock Ownership Plans (ESOPs), many large firms sold large ESOP- related issues just before the new tax laws became effective (July of that year). More than $7 billion of ESOP notes were issued in the private market in June 1989. More generally, corporations have relied upon the private market when funds were needed before a time¬consuming public registration could be completed. Often these transactions are to finance acquisitions, and in many instances the issues are sold with registration rights, which places in interest rate penalty on the issuer if the securities are not registered publicly within a specified period of time.

Another special circumstance leading firms to use the private market involves financings requiring nonstandard or customized features, such as delayed disbursements or staggered takedowns.

In general, selling securities with such specialized terms in the public market is not possible, but investors in private placements often have the flexibility to accommodate issuers' preferences.

Firms with privately placed, medium-term note programs may also be considered a group that issues in the private market for reasons related mainly to regulatory and practical restrictions in the public markets. Medium-term notes have made up an increasing share of total private placement issuance over the past four years. In 1991, for example, medium- term note issuance totaled $6.2 billion, representing 8.3 percent of total private bond issuance. However, this amount was small relative to public medium-term note issuance in 1991, which totaled $73.5 billion. Most firms that have private, medium-term note programs are either private or foreign firms that issue no public securities or public firms that issue privately while waiting to establish a public program.

Fixed Costs of Issuance, Issue Size, and Choice of Market

Besides information problems and regulatory requirements, fixed costs of issuance can affect a borrower's choice of market. Most private placements are for amounts between $10 million and $100 million. Focusing first on the tradeoff that can be decisive for issues around $100 million in size, issuance expenses are generally lower for private than for public securities, primarily because they are not registered with the SEC and because they are not are underwritten. Public issuers incur both registration and underwriting expenses. For large issues that are not information problematic, however, the higher fixed costs of a public offering are often offset by the availability of lower interest rates, which reflect the greater liquidity of public bonds and the smaller costs of credit analysis that public lenders bear.

Consequently, a company that could issue in either market would find, all else being equal, that the choice hinged upon the size of the offering.

For issues smaller than some size cutoff, lower issuance costs make the private market less expensive; for larger issues, lower yields make the public market less expensive. Currently, market participants place the break-even point for the two markets between $75 million and $100 million.

At the other end of the spectrum, private placements below $10 million are relatively uncommon for three reasons. First, private placements involve some fixed costs of issuance, which can make total costs of small private issues high. Also, most buyers of private placements would demand high interest rates on small issues to cover their fixed costs of due diligence and loan monitoring. Finally, prospective issuers of small amounts tend to be smaller than the average private market borrower. Such issuers may be too information problematic for private market lenders, whose monitoring capacity is not so high as that of banks and some other lenders. Consequently, as noted above, small companies tend to rely on other sources of funds, one being the bank loan market. As in the private placement market, fees can cause the effective interest rates on bank loans to vary inversely with loan size; nonetheless, for most small borrowers, bank loans are preferable to private placements.

Because mainly small and medium-sized companies are information problematic and because such companies typically borrow small or moderate amounts, differential fixed costs of issuance as well as the need for an information- intensive lender lead such companies to borrow in the private placement or bank loan markets rather than the public market. The most important factor in determining the market in which a firm issue, however, seems to be the extent of the information problems the firm poses for lenders.

Factors Influencing Market Choice

Apart from gaining access to credit markets through financial intermediaries, information- problematic firms often gain other advantages from issuing private placements. Borrowers have the opportunity to establish relationships with lenders, the terms of the securities can be tailored to some degree to suit the borrowers' needs, the advancement of funds can be staggered or delayed, and confidentiality concerning the borrowers' financial condition and business operations can be maintained. Restrictive covenants, however, impose costly restrictions on borrowers and thus are seen as a disadvantage. In addition, prepayment penalties eliminate borrowers' opportunity to refinance the bonds at a cost saving, regardless of the level of interest rates.

Nevertheless, medium-sized, or hard-to-understand borrowers in search of long-term, fixed-rate funds are often willing to trade off the risk control features of private bonds against their perceived benefits.

From Stock Prices Evidence

Previous studies of the reaction of stock prices to announcements that firms had placed bonds privately support the hypothesis that the private placement market is information intensive. In one study, Szewczyk and Varma (1991) hypothesize that, if a company is information problematic, its stock price should rise in response to the announcement of a private placement. Stock investors might view the private placement as a signal that the firm is more creditworthy inasmuch as institutions with access to private information are willing to invest in the firm. If stock investors view the successful placement of private debt as a signal that the firm is engaging in value-enhancing projects, they are likely to bid up the price of the firm's stock. In addition, stock investors may realize that the private placement probably results in the monitoring of the firm's management by additional lenders.

For a sample of public utility companies issuing private placements between 1963 and 1986, Szewczyk and Varma found that their stock prices, on average, significantly exceeded the predicted change after the announcement of a private placement. Moreover, the greatest positive response was shown by utilities that had not issued debt publicly, that is, those for which the least amount of public information would have been available. As a check on the results, Szewczyk and Varma also examined stock prices of utilities that had not placed debt privately.

In response to the utilities' announcements of public debt offerings, the changes in their stock prices fell short, on average, of predicted changes.

Research by Bailey and Mullineaux (1989) and Vora (1991) also supports a conclusion that private placement issuers tend to be information problematic. In contrast, James (1987) and Banning and James (1989) find a negative stock price response, but it comes for private placements used to pay down bank loans. In such situations, the number of lenders monitoring management may not increase, and the intensity of monitoring might decrease. Taken as a whole, the results support a conclusion that private issuers are information problematic, but not as problematic on average as bank borrowers.

Differences between Firms Issuing in the Public, Private, and Bank Loan Markets

To summarize the preceding discussion, borrowers' access to debt markets is apparently closely related to firm size, with size mainly a proxy for the degree of information problems that borrowers pose for lenders. Broadly speaking, very information-problematic companies without collateral may be unable to borrow even from an information-intensive lender. Such companies, which are typically small, may be forced to rely on venture capital or on other forms of equity finance. Small firms that are less information problematic or those that can provide collateral are confined largely to the bank and finance company loan markets for debt financing. Even fewer problematic firms, which are typically medium-sized, also have access to the private placement market. Large corporations can borrow in any of these markets and in the public bond market. Besides size of the firm, other characteristics, especially those related to the nature and size of the financing, are important in determining a firm's choice of credit market.

Empirical evidence supports these assertions. We analyzed the characteristics of firms classified according to a hierarchy of access to the public, private, and bank loan markets and found a pattern of firm sizes and other characteristics consistent with the explanation of borrowers' choice of market that focuses on the different information problems posed by different firms. However, borrower size is also correlated with issue size and with observable borrower risk, so the observed difference in sizes of firms with different levels of access is also potentially consistent with explanations based on issuance costs or risk. To evaluate the relative importance of the three explanations, we looked at several other firm characteristics that are plausibly correlated either with the degree of information problems or with observable risk.

We employed an indirect approach in identifying the access of actual firms to the three markets, since access is not directly observable. We combined information on corporations in COMPUSTAT with data on private placements from the IDD database. Corporations in COMPUSTAT with a long-term credit rating are assumed to have access to the public bond market, inasmuch as they must have issued corporate bonds at some time to have received a bond rating; those without a rating are assumed to lack access to the public market. In 1989, 1,149 corporations in COMPUSTAT had ratings and thus constitute the public market group, that is, those corporations with the ability to raise funds in public debt markets. To form a group of firms with access to the private placement market but not to the public market, companies listed in the IDD private placement database as issuing in 1989 were matched with those in COMPUSTAT that had no credit rating. The cross¬matching of the two databases yielded a total of 113 such companies, which make up what is called the private market group. Those firms in COMPUSTAT that in 1989 had neither a credit rating nor outstanding long-term debt but that did have some short-term debt outstanding were assumed to be constrained to borrow only from banks (or other, bank-like intermediaries such as finance companies); this collection of firms is called the bank group and contains 472 members. Finally, those firms in COMPUSTAT that had neither a credit rating nor any outstanding debt (short or long term, except for trade debt) in 1989 were assumed to be shut out of all three debt markets. This collection of firms is called the equity group and consists of 613 firms.

This method of classifying firms is far from perfect for various reasons. First, and perhaps most important, implicit in the definition of each group is an assumption that a company cannot tap a particular debt market if it has not actually done.

This assumption is clearly not correct in all cases. For example, several firms classified in the bank group probably could have issued in the private or public bond markets on standard terms but simply chose not to do so. Firms that issued private placements before 1989 but not in 1989 are less likely to fall in the bank group because such firms probably still showed long-term debt on their balance sheets in 1989. Second, according to the bank group definition, the presence of short- term debt on the balance sheet indicates the firm's ability to tap the bank loan market. However, COMPUSTAT's definition of short-term debt includes loans from various lenders: loans payable to stockholders, officers of the company, parents, subsidiaries, and brokerage companies as well as loans payable to banks, finance companies, and other intermediaries. Our aim is to include in the bank group all firms that have access to banks or bank-like intermediaries, but several firms without such access were probably misclassified (they should be in the equity group) because they had loans outstanding from stockholders or other non-intermediary sources. Third, many equity groups firms may have had bank lines of credit that were simply unused at the end of their 1989 fiscal years. 57 Fourth, the presence of a credit rating in COMPUSTAT implies only that a firm once had access to the public bond market, not that it had access in 1989.

The private market, bank, and equity groups are also undoubtedly biased selections of firms because only those firms that appear on the COMPUSTAT tapes have been selected. COMPUSTAT's bias toward large firms means that the firms in these three groups are likely larger on average than corresponding groups of firms for the economy as a whole. Other characteristics may show some bias as well. However, the bias probably makes observed differences across groups less dramatic. Consequently, any differences found in the analysis are unlikely to be the result of this sampling bias.

Finally, the criteria used to define the four groups focus on the characteristics of the firm, not on the characteristics of the debt issue. As mentioned earlier, some firms that could readily issue straight debt in the public market may be constrained to the private market for more complicated issues such as some leases or project financings. We address this issue later in this section.

Despite these classification problems and biases, we believe our method of classifying firms is on the whole roughly accurate and that the distinctions that are revealed are economically meaningful.

The firm characteristics examined include the size of the firm, measured by total assets, sales, and market value of equity. We also looked at the three-year growth rate of sales, return on assets, (measured by operating income before depreciation divided by total assets), research and development (R&D) expenditures as a percentage of sales, the fixed-asset ratio, the ratio of total debt to assets, and the interest coverage ratio.

Differences in firm size across groups, measured by total assets, total sales, or market value of equity, are pronounced. Firms in the public market group are much larger than firms in the private market group, which in turn are very much larger than firms in the bank or equity groups. For example, mean assets of companies in the public market group are $6.3 billion, considerably larger than the mean of $3.4 billion for firms in the private market group. The means for the bank and equity groups are even smaller at $40 million. These differences in means are all statistically significant at the 1 percent level. The medians have a similar relationship among the three groups. The statistics for three other variables that are plausibly correlated with the degree of information problems posed by firms: the ratio of R&D expenditures to sales, the fixed-asset ratio, and a three- year average growth rate for sales. Many economists have used R&D expenditures as a proxy for the potential severity of agency problems between shareholders and debtholders. The risk implicit in research and development cannot be easily monitored by outsiders, including debtholders, as a firm with large R&D expenditures has wide scope for discretionary behavior. For example, such a firm may require intensive monitoring by debtholders to ensure that it is working on a mundane research project with a moderate but fairly sure payoff rather than a longshot with a high payoff. Intensive monitoring may be required to ensure that the firm is not underinvesting in projects with positive net present values (Myers, 1977). R&D- intensive companies, being inherently more information problematic than other firms, may therefore find banks more receptive to providing financing because banks can monitor more intensively than lenders in the public markets. The evidence provided by this variable on the intensity of monitoring in the private placement market generally conforms with our hypothesis about differences in the degree of information problems across the four groups. Mean R&D intensity is higher in the private placement market than in the public market, although the medians are about the same. The significantly higher R&D intensity for the bank and equity groups than that for the private market group indicates that issuers in the former groups tend to require significantly more monitoring by lenders than do issuers of private placements.

A similar hierarchy of information problems is suggested by the fixed-asset ratios. Firms with a large percentage of fixed assets may have fewer information problems than other firms for two reasons. First, they may be able to offer some of their fixed plant and equipment as collateral to potential creditors. Second, monitoring the sale of fixed assets or their transformation from one use to another may be easier than it is for more liquid assets. The more of a firm's assets that are fixed, therefore, the smaller may be the scope for shareholders to engage in wealth-transferring investment projects.

As one moves from the public to the private to the bank and finally to the equity group, the decline in fixed-asset ratios implies that information problems increase. The higher fixed-asset ratio for the bank group compared with that for the equity group suggests that a small firm's ability to provide fixed assets as collateral may be a factor in its ability to obtain bank loans.

Sales growth rates may also be correlated with information problems in that high growth may be a sign of entry into new lines of business or of being in lines of business that are in rapidly developing markets. Both situations offer more scope for agency problems to surface during the life of a debt contract. The evidence from this variable, however, is weaker than that from R&D intensity and the fixed-asset ratio: The mean is significantly smaller for firms in the public group than for those in the private group, a finding consistent with private issuers requiring more monitoring; the median is smaller as well. Values for the private group do not differ significantly from those for the bank and equity groups, however, and the medians display an uneven pattern.

On the whole, the results for the three variables conform with our hypothesis about the differing degree of information problems posed by the four groups of firms. They also accord with the remarks of market participants, who asserted that buyers of private placements, especially the larger life insurance companies, engage in organized and active monitoring, although their monitoring programs are typically not so intensive as those of banks.

Average return on assets and two measures of leverage, total-debt-to-asset ratios, and interest coverage ratios, are indicators of observable credit risk. information problems and observable credit risk are separate concepts, and in principle there is no reason that the pattern of credit risk should be different in information¬intensive and non-information- intensive markets. In practice, however, both are related to borrower size.

Caution should be used in interpreting the differences between the bank and equity groups and the other groups in the measures of leverage, as firms in the former groups either had no long-term debt outstanding or no debt at all on their balance sheets (according to COMPUSTAT and ignoring trade debt). Thus, zeros will appear in either the numerator or the denominator of the ratios for many equity groups firms, making the ratios poor measures of the riskiness of these firms and influencing the mean and median values for the groups.

A comparison of ratios for the public and private placement groups indicates that differences in credit risk may not be as great as differences in information problems. Both the mean and median debt-to-asset ratios and the return on assets are similar for the two groups. Median interest- coverage ratios are also similar, but the mean interest-coverage ratio is significantly higher for the public group. The implication is that private placements issuers may be somewhat riskier as a class, but not a great deal riskier, than public bond issuers. Comparing ratios for the private placement and bank groups, the means of the three ratios differ significantly; the medians also differ as predicted except for the debt-to-asset ratio. It appears that members of the bank group pose larger observable credit risks for lenders.

On the whole, these results accord well with the remarks of market participants, who often described private issuers as "solid companies" that have taken a major step in "graduating" from having access only to the bank loan market but that are typically "not quite ready" to issue in the public bond market. Some investors also indicated that their historical experience of loss on private placements and public bonds was virtually identical within credit-rating categories. The statistics presented here and the remarks of participants offer little support for a hypothesis that low observable credit risk is the primary requirement for a borrower to have access to the public market, instead of only the private placement and bank loan markets. The existence of the public junk bond market and the fact that contract terms, especially covenants, and lender due diligence and monitoring activities differ across the public and private markets for borrowers with the same bond ratings also imply that information problems are a more important determinant of market access than observable credit risk.

In sum, if the groups of firms analyzed here are representative of borrowers' access to debt markets, then their characteristics are broadly consistent with our explanation of the factors influencing borrowers' choice of debt market. Corporations able to borrow in the public markets tend to be large and to pose relatively few information problems for lenders; thus, they can borrow from a wide variety of lenders. Companies issuing in the private but not the public market are smaller and appear to be more information problematic; however, they apparently do not represent substantially greater observable credit risks. Such companies must be served by information-intensive lenders. The companies confined to the bank loan market or to equity markets are much smaller, are more information problematic, and pose larger pure credit risks.

Consequently, they require the greatest degree of due diligence and loan monitoring by lenders, or they are unable to issue debt at all. The information problems associated with smaller and medium-sized firms and their increased need for information-intensive lenders appear to be the major reasons for the size pattern observed among the three groups and for the differential access of firms to credit markets.

Companies Issuing in Both the Private and the Public Markets

As mentioned earlier, some firms that could readily issue straight debt in the public market may be constrained to the private market for more complicated issues, such as leases or project financings. To obtain evidence regarding this hypothesis, we examined differences in private issues between our private market group and a fifth group of firms that issue in the private market even though they have previously tapped the public market for funds. This group, called the public-private group, consists of those firms that are listed in the IDD database as having issued a private placement in 1989 and listed on the COMPUSTAT tape as having a bond rating. It comprises 109 firms, with 175 issues of private debt in 1989.

Several differences exist between the private debt issues of firms in the private market group and those in the public-private group. The much larger average size of private placement issues by the public-private firms than that of the private market group firms reflects the much larger size of firm in the former group. In addition, the mix of securities issued by the private market firms differs significantly from that of the public- private group in terms of their credit analysis requirements. We define "complex" securities to be equipment trusts, lease-backed bonds, leveraged leases, receivables- backed bonds, and variable and floating rate notes. Complex securities appear in the public market, but in many cases, they require investors to engage in sophisticated and intensive credit analysis. We define "simple" debt securities to be senior securities, secured notes, mortgage- backed notes, debentures, and medium-term notes. Simple securities likely require less in the way of due diligence and monitoring. Measured by the number of issuers and by the dollar amount issued, the percentage of total private issuance in the form of complex securities was much higher in 1989 for public- private group firms than for private market group firms. Conversely, a much higher percentage of total private issuance by private market firms in 1989 was in the form of simple debt. 61 This evidence supports the hypothesis that firms with access to the public market may choose to issue more complex securities in the private market, where the capacity of investors for credit analysis is greater.

The average size of simple and complex issues for the two groups of firms is consistent with the proposition that issuance cost is of secondary importance in determining market choice by borrowers (last two rows of table 6). The average issue size for complex private placements was $576.5 million, suggesting that on the basis of issuance costs alone the public market would have been the appropriate choice. That they were issued in the private market indicates that due diligence and loan monitoring requirements were such that only information-intensive lenders would buy the issues.

Simple securities issued by the public-private group could be issued in either the public or the private market because they require relatively low levels of due diligence and monitoring by lenders. In this case, issuance costs are likely to be a dominant consideration. The average issue size of $50.8 million for the simple securities issued by the public-private group in the private market is consistent with this notion, because the private market reportedly offers lower total costs for issues of that size.

The marked differences between firm characteristics and loan characteristics for the various groups support the hypothesis that firms have differential access to the three markets according to the information problems they pose for lenders. At one end of the scale are small, relatively unknown firms posing significant information problems that require extensive due diligence or loan monitoring by lenders. These firms tend to have access only to relatively short-term loans provided by banks and other bank-like intermediaries, which have the staff and expertise to undertake information- intensive lending and which limit borrowers' risk-taking through tight covenants or collateral in loan agreements.

Somewhat less information-problematic, typically larger borrowers can issue in the private placement market. These borrowers must still be served by an information-intensive lender, but they pose fewer problems than the average bank borrower. They can issue longer-term debt with somewhat looser covenants than those in bank loans.

Finally, well-known, typically larger firms that are not information problematic and that have straightforward financings can issue in the public debt markets, where lenders perform little due diligence and loan monitoring and where covenants are relatively few in number and loose in nature. The pattern is evidence that the various debt markets are imperfect substitutes for one another, which implies that breakdowns or failures in one market may have material effects on firms that rely on that market for a major part of their financing needs, even if other markets are functioning normally.

CHAPTER 3

Private Placement Market Lenders

Although various institutions hold some traditional private placements in their portfolios, life insurance companies purchase the great majority of them. For example, for a sample of 351 placements issued during 1990-92, life insurance companies purchased 83 percent of dollar volume, whereas the next largest type of investor, foreign banks, purchased only 3.6 percent. Lending in the private placement market is also concentrated in the hands of a relatively few lenders. Although the sample lists 315 separate investors, most participated in only one deal or in a few deals and bought only small amounts. The top twenty investors were life insurance companies and accounted for 56 percent of dollar volume.

The concentration of private placement lending in the hands of a relatively few lenders and a few types of lender has probably occurred for four reasons. First, the large proportion of information- problematic borrowers in the traditional private market necessitates that major buyers of private placements be intermediaries. Intermediaries can capture economies of scale in due diligence and monitoring and can also build and maintain over long periods the reputations for fair dealing that are important when debt contracts must include covenants.

Second, financial intermediaries tend to specialize in a few liability-side lines of business (for example, banks mainly take deposits) at least partly because of regulatory restrictions. Given such specialization, the natural tendency of lenders to seek superior risk-adjusted returns will lead to specialization on the asset side. Different debt instruments are associated with different patterns of risks, and different lenders have different abilities to implement a cost-effective and appropriate set of risk control measures in order to earn superior risk-adjusted returns on any given type of asset. For example, banks' short-term deposit liabilities lead them to make short-term loans, whereas insurance companies' longer-term liabilities lead them to purchase longer-term assets. The risks most commonly associated with traditional private placements of debt are credit risk, asset concentration risk, interest rate risk, and liquidity risk. Extensive credit evaluation and monitoring are required to control credit risk in private placements, whereas appropriate diversification can control asset concentration risk. Interest rate risk may be controlled by matching private placements with liabilities of similar duration, or other hedges. With regard to liquidity risk, if a lender holds private placements, its liabilities must not be redeemable on demand, or other parts of its portfolio must be sufficiently liquid to meet any likely withdrawals. The relative efficiency with which different classes of financial intermediary can undertake to control these risks, as well as legal and regulatory constraints, determines the institutional pattern of investments in private placements. Although many financial intermediaries can effectively control the credit and asset concentration risks associated with private placements, life insurance companies are especially well positioned to control the liquidity and interest rate risks.

A third reason for the concentration of private placement lending is the concentrated structure of the insurance and related markets. At the end of 1991, the twenty largest life insurance companies held 51 percent of industry assets. Because these companies have a large volume of funds to invest, their domination of the private placement market is natural. A final reason for concentration is that large lenders have an advantage in obtaining private placements because their large volume of investments permits them to participate in the market continuously, giving them up-to-date information about the state of the market. Little detailed information on investors in private placements is publicly available.

Consequently, much of our discussion is based on interviews with market participants. To summarize this information, life insurers buy a broad spectrum of private placements, but many of them focus on senior, unsecured debt. Finance companies are also said to be significant buyers of private debt, but they tend to specialize in high- risk investments and, consequently, require that borrowers provide collateral and equity kickers, such as warrants or convertible bonds. They have developed special expertise in due diligence and monitoring involving collateral and equity features. Though commercial banks have the capabilities for credit analysis, they are not significant buyers of private placements, probably because their short-term, liquid, floating-rate liabilities are not well matched by private bonds. Regulatory and other restraints prevent or discourage major investors in public bonds, such as most pension funds and mutual funds, from investing heavily in private bonds.

Life Insurance Companies

Market participants estimate that life insurers purchase between 50 percent and 80 percent of new issue volume each year. At year-end 1991, life insurers held $212 billion of private placements in their general accounts, representing 26 percent of their total bond holdings and 16 percent of their general account assets.

The twenty largest insurance companies, as measured by total assets, accounted for 68 percent of industry holdings of private placements at the end of 1992. Furthermore, for this group, private placements were 39 percent of total bond holdings and 22 percent of general account assets. The next eighty largest insurers account for most of the remaining industry holdings of private placements, and within this group, several companies have sizable portfolios.

Some idea of how the life insurance industry allocates its funds among different classes of private bonds can be obtained from the ACLI Investment Bulletin, which provides data on the composition of new commitments of funds to private placements by major insurance companies. Life insurance companies strongly prefer fixed-rate private placements: In 1992, more than 97 percent of their commitments were fixed rate. Securitized instruments, mainly mortgage-backed securities, were 13 percent of commitments although, as discussed earlier, a much larger fraction probably carried collateral. Insurers invest primarily in medium- to long-term maturities; less than 10 percent of their 1992 commitments had an average life of three years or less, with more than half having average lives between five and ten years.

This concentration on medium- to long-term, fixed-rate debt is sensible because such securities can easily be matched with the life insurance industry's long-term, fixed-rate liabilities. Many private placements also have sinking fund provisions that further enable insurers to match the cash flow of their investments with that of their liabilities. The strong call protection that is typical of private placements also facilitates matching. 65 Life insurance companies buy private placements from firms in all sectors of the economy. Most tend to diversify across a broad range of industries, although many have favorite industries in which they have a particular expertise. In 1992 78 percent of their total commitments went to the nonfinancial sector, with just over 30 percent going to manufacturing, 8 percent to the oil, gas, and mining industries, and another 20 percent to the utilities, communication, and transportation sectors. Life insurance companies have sharply increased their purchases of securities issued by foreign companies, or U.S. subsidiaries of foreign companies, to over 7 percent in 1992 from less than 3 percent of total commitments in 1990.

The large insurers' investment in risk-control technology is extensive. Most of these insurers have large staffs of credit analysts, who evaluate the credit quality of potential issuers and monitor the health of firms to which credit has been extended. Most conduct a quarterly review of each private bond held in their portfolios, with a more formal annual or semiannual review. Violations of covenants or requests for waivers of covenants generate further reviews. The costs of risk- control operations are covered by the higher risk- adjusted yield of private placements relative to public bonds, which require little or no active monitoring by security holders. The private market provides borrowers willing to compensate the lender for these risk-control services.

The large investment in credit evaluation and monitoring leads most large insurance companies to concentrate on more complex credits; however, strategies vary even among these companies.

Besides dominating the straight debt sector of the market, life insurers buy other types of private securities, such as convertible debt or asset-backed bonds, though their share of these sectors is somewhat lower. In terms of credit quality, insurers focus primarily on securities rated A and BBB. At the end of 1992, around 17 percent of total private bonds held by the twenty largest companies were rated below investment grade; however, substantial variation exists, with some companies having up to 38 per- cent of their private portfolio in below-investment- grade bonds and others having almost none at all. Securities in this credit range, particularly those rated just below investment grade (which insurers often refer to as Baa4 securities), are favored by those insurance companies attempting to gain maximum advantage from their credit analysis and monitoring skills. These insurance companies like to take advantage of the large difference in yields between investment-grade and below-investment-grade credits by lending to strong BB-rated companies. However, others are more conservative and focus solely on issues rated A or higher.

According to market participants, smaller insurers typically have much less extensive risk-control technology at their disposal. They therefore tend to concentrate on higher-quality, less-complex credits. They also may participate in deals that larger insurance companies have already committed to, using the presence of these larger insurers as a signal that the deal is a favorable one.

Most insurance companies rely heavily on agents for prospective transactions, although some direct lending occurs between an insurer and its existing borrowers. Only the very largest insurance companies originate new transactions on a regular basis, and only one insurer syndicates private bonds. The largest insurers generally prefer to be the sole source of funds for an issuer. However, many issues are larger than the maximum amount that individual insurers permit to be lent to one borrower; a typical issue may have up to a half dozen insurance companies funding it. Insurers typically fund between 5 and 20 percent of the deals that are marketed to them.

Most large insurers invest in both public and private bonds, and they have allocation mechanisms to alter the flow of money into these markets as spreads change in the two markets. Until recently, the groups within large insurance companies responsible for purchasing private and public bonds were usually separated; however, some companies have recently combined the groups. Market participants report that many medium-sized insurers have for some time used a single group to make all investments in bonds.

Finance Companies

Finance companies have traditionally participated in the lower-rated or mezzanine sector of the private bond market, specializing in collateralized debt or debt with equity kickers. Rates in this sector of the market may be fixed or floating.

Finance companies' choice of this market sector follows naturally from their historical concentration in secured or asset-based lending. Returns on private placements required by finance companies are generally well in excess of the yields on the less risky, straight bonds purchased by insurance companies.

According to market participants, the participation of finance companies in the private market is much more concentrated than that of insurance companies. Among the twenty largest finance companies, only a half dozen or so provide a significant volume of funds, although some others are attempting to expand their presence in the market. Outside the top twenty, few finance companies participate at all.

Pension Funds

Pension funds, which are significant investors in publicly issued corporate bonds, have not been big buyers of private placements, except for a few state pensions funds. Market participants suggest several reasons. First, many pension funds have charters preventing them from investing in below-investment-grade or illiquid assets. Although in practice some higher-rated private bonds may be more liquid than some public bonds, market participants generally consider private placements to be illiquid. Second, few state or corporate pension funds are currently staffed with the credit analysts and other personnel that would allow them to become direct investors in private placements. Instead, staffing is directed toward public market investments, which require much less credit analysis. A decision to hire the necessary staff and install the expensive internal monitoring systems to support direct investment in private placements would require a long-term commitment to the private market by the pension manager. Few pension fund managers thus far have been willing to so commit. Even if they should wish to do so, state pension funds face problems in hiring the necessary personnel. Staff size and salaries are generally controlled by the state legislatures, and increasing the size of credit analysis staffs is thus cumbersome and time- consuming.

As an alternative to direct investment, some pension funds have turned to money managers, often insurance companies. Indirect investments, however, are on a fairly small scale, no doubt partly because pension fund managers are reluctant to invest even indirectly in a market with which they are unfamiliar. The private market operates largely in conformance with unwritten, informal rules enforced by the desire of the major agents and buyers involved to maintain their reputations. To investors that are outsiders, the way the market operates may thus be hard to understand, which may inhibit them from risking their money there. Also, insurance companies themselves, who would be the primary source of the managerial resources necessary for any large-scale activity in this area, have been reluctant to set up separate account private placement funds financed with institutional money. They apparently see little investor interest in such funds or do not wish to interrupt the flow of private placements to the company itself. Furthermore, market participants report that investor experience with at least one separate account fund has not been good because the managing insurance company, lacking a stake in the separate account investments, did not perform adequate monitoring.

Banks

Banks, which are information-intensive lenders, might also be expected to have interest in the types of securities offered in the private market. However, for several reasons they seldom buy private placements. First, banks' liabilities are not long term and are not as well matched with private bonds on the asset side as they are with short-term, floating-rate loans. Of course, the swap market can be used to turn fixed-rate assets into floating-rate, but longer-term swaps are expensive. Second, the looser covenants on private placements relative to bank loans may make some banks uncomfortable.

Bank purchases of private placements are subject to some regulatory restrictions, which are described in appendix C. Bank holding companies may purchase privately placed debt securities without restriction. Banks themselves may also purchase them but must place them in a loan account and follow traditional underwriting procedures. The latter requirement means that banks must evaluate and document the credit worthiness of the borrower as they would with any bank loan. As credit analysis is the norm in the private placement market, such evaluation and documentation do not appear to be onerous requirements. Some issuers attempt to create interest among banks and life insurance companies by constructing offerings that include both private bonds and loans, which are identical in their terms except for the classification of the instrument.

Other Investors

Other investors in private bonds include mutual funds, foreign banks, endowment funds, and some very wealthy individuals, but the combined market share of these participants is quite small. Mutual funds are restricted to holding no more than 15 percent of their assets in the form of illiquid securities. An exception exists for private placements purchased pursuant to Rule 144A. For such securities, the mutual funds' boards of directors may classify the securities as liquid if they determine that the securities are generally as liquid as comparable publicly traded bonds. Mutual funds have recently increased their investments in private placements, especially underwritten Rule 144A securities, so current restrictions may in the future be constraints. In the mid-1980s, Japanese banks aggressively bought private bonds, but since then they have disappeared from the market.

A capacity for due diligence and loan monitoring is a prerequisite for a significant volume of direct investment in private placements by a lender. Life insurance companies, finance companies, banks, and a few other financial institutions have this capability. However, life insurers dominate the private debt market, partly because they have large pools of funds suitable for investment in longer- term, fixed-rate, illiquid securities. Insurance companies also have a long history of lending directly to middle-market firms that has allowed them to develop expertise and cost-effective risk-control technologies. This expertise may constitute a barrier to entry for other financial institutions, including most pension funds, which might otherwise seem to be suited to lending in this market. Regulatory and other obstacles also discourage pension funds and mutual funds from participating heavily in the market. Banks have the necessary expertise in credit monitoring but for several reasons have not found private placements to be suitable investments. As in other credit markets, finance companies have carved out a niche in the private market for higher-risk borrowers. This segment constitutes a small part of the overall market, but it is one in which the insurance companies have little interest.

Some market participants feel that, over the long term, pension funds will overcome the obstacles that have precluded their large-scale participation to date and will be much more important providers of funds in this market, much as they have replaced life insurance companies as the major source of finance in the private equity market The immense growth of their assets projected for the future may force pension plans to consider investments in markets new to them.

However, the information-intensive nature of the traditional private market is unlikely to change; so, if pension funds are to be a larger source of finance, they will likely become so through indirect investments in funds managed by insurance companies. The alternative is for pension funds themselves to acquire the capacity for conducting due diligence and monitoring.

The Theory of Financial Intermediation, and The Structure of Capital Markets Of Private Placements

As previously discussed, contract terms and borrower and lender characteristics differ systematically across major debt markets. Privately and publicly issued bonds tend to have long terms and fixed rates, whereas bank loans tend to have short terms and floating rates. Public issues and issuers are the largest on average, and bank loans and bank borrowers are the smallest. On average, public issues are the least risky, private placements are riskier, and bank loans are riskier still. Public issuers tend to be well known; private placement issuers tend to be less well known; and bank borrowers tend to be companies for which relatively little information is available publicly. Public issues rarely include collateral and have few restrictive covenants. In traditional private placements, collateral is not uncommon, and covenants often impose significant restrictions on borrowers. Bank loans, in contrast, tend both to be secured and to have tight covenants. The terms of public issues are rarely renegotiated, whereas those of most private placements are renegotiated at least once, and those of bank loans are frequently renegotiated. Public issues are typically liquid, whereas most private placements and bank loans are illiquid. Investors in public securities carry out relatively little due diligence and monitoring of borrowers. Investors in bank loans and private placements perform significant amounts of due diligence and loan monitoring.

Most private placement lending is done by a single type of financial intermediary, life insurance companies.

This section offers an integrated explanation for these patterns, elements of which have been mentioned in previous sections. The explanation is centered on hypotheses that borrowers pose a spectrum of information problems for lenders and that lenders address such problems through due diligence at loan origination and loan monitoring thereafter. Firms that are not information problematic can borrow in any market but generally find costs to be lowest in the public bond (and commercial paper) markets. Information- problematic firms find it optimal to negotiate debt contracts that include certain kinds of covenants and collateral and to deal with lenders having a capacity for due diligence and loan monitoring.

Such lenders also can flexibly renegotiate the contracts, which is efficient since covenants are frequently violated.

Such contracts are not well suited to the public markets that exist today; instead they are issued in the bank loan and private placement markets. Lenders in these markets are almost always financial intermediaries, and they tend to focus their investments in assets that match the rate and maturity structure of their liabilities. Correlations among several factors—the degree of information problems posed by borrowers, the borrowers' size, their risk, and the size of the loan— account for borrowers being smaller and riskier on average and loans smaller on average in such information- intensive markets than those in the public markets.

The differences between the average borrower from banks and the average issuer of private placements arise mainly because monitoring and risk control mechanisms involving covenants and collateral are less reliable the longer the average life of a loan is. Such mechanisms are most important in loans to very information- problematic borrowers; these borrowers can obtain long-term loans only at high rates, if at all. Thus, they tend to borrow in the shorter-term market, causing the average severity of information problems posed by borrowers to be highest there.

This explanation accounts for more of the features of the U.S. financial system than do traditional explanations that focus mainly on regulation and considerations of asset-liability matching as causal factors. It raises many new questions, however. Why must lenders to information-problematic borrowers be intermediaries? How do due diligence and loan monitoring mitigate risks associated with information problems? What is the role of covenants and collateral? Why are these risk-control mechanisms less effective for long-term loans? Why would a borrower agree to a contract with tighter rather than looser covenants? Why are covenants frequently violated and renegotiated, and why is a lender's reputation for flexibility in renegotiation important? Why is information-intensive debt illiquid? Why is the public market ill-suited to information-intensive lending (what is to prevent public market lenders from acquiring capacity in due diligence and loan monitoring)? What complex of characteristics is required to make a lender competitive in an information-intensive debt market?

Most of these questions have been addressed at least to some extent by existing financial theory. In the rest of this section, we review and extend relevant areas of financial theory to answer these questions and to provide a sense of the foundations of this study. We find existing individual theories of covenants and financial intermediation to be inadequate as a basis for a theory of financial structure. We propose a merging and an extension of the two bodies of theory in the form of a "covenant-monitoring-renegotiation" (CMR) paradigm in order to answer to the questions posed earlier. We evaluate the consistency of the paradigm with some recent research in empirical finance and graphically relate borrowers and capital markets on an information continuum.

Asymmetric Information, Contracting, and the Theory of Covenants

Two imperfections of capital markets are at the heart of many of the contracting problems that shape debt markets. First, the interests of bondholders and stockholders of borrowing firms are not always aligned; second, parties to financial contracts are not likely to be equally informed about the characteristics of the issuing firm. The informational advantage borrowers have over lenders leads to two kinds of bondholder- stockholder conflict. First, once a debt contract is signed, borrowers have incentives to expropriate wealth from lenders (moral hazard). Second, before a contract is signed, potential borrowers have incentives to understate the risks they will pose for lenders, including moral hazard risks. A simple example of moral hazard risk is provided by Black (1976), who noted that "there is no easier way for a company to escape the burden of a debt than to pay out all of its assets in the form of a dividend, and leave the creditors holding an empty shell" . In the absence of sufficiently powerful constraints or capacity for lender monitoring and enforcement capacity, such actions may be either unobservable by the firm's bond- holders or beyond their control. Smith and Warner (1979) identify four major kinds of moral hazard that lenders must control:

Dividend payment. If a firm issues bonds and the bonds are priced assuming the firm will maintain its dividend policy, the value of the bonds is reduced by raising the dividend rate and financing the increase by reducing investment. At the limit, if the firm sells all its assets and pays a liquidating dividend to the stockholders, the bondholders are left with worth- less claims.

Claim dilution. If the firm sells bonds, and the bonds are priced assuming that no additional debt will be issued, the value of the bondholders' claims is reduced by issuing additional debt of the same or higher priority.

Asset substitution. If a firm sells bonds for the stated purpose of engaging in low variance projects and the bonds are valued at prices commensurate with that low risk, the value of the stockholders' equity rises and the value of the bondholders' claim is reduced by substituting projects which increase the firm's variance rate.

Underinvestment. Myers (1977) suggests that a substantial portion of the value of the firm is composed of intangible assets in the form of future investment opportunities. A firm with outstanding bonds can have incentives to reject projects which have a positive net present value if the benefit from accepting the project accrues to the bondholders.

Covenants may alter the relationship between bondholders and stockholders in two fundamental ways. First, covenants affect the relationship when the borrowing firm is in financial distress by providing lenders with a mechanism for early intervention. This intervention may take one of several forms: forced bankruptcy, a renegotiated restructuring, or the imposition of additional constraints on firm behavior. This can be viewed as the role of covenants ex post, which is to permit these interventions after the consequences of the firm's actions have been revealed.

Second, and possibly more important, is the role of covenants ex ante. Debt contracts that include covenants can effectively constrain the ability of stockholders to engage in strategies designed to expropriate wealth from bondholders or otherwise to engage in actions that are detrimental to bondholders. Smith and Warner document that covenants of the kind observed in private placements and bank loan contracts can mitigate bondholder-stockholder conflicts. They also demonstrate that contracting is not a zero-sum game. Terms of contracts affect not only the distribution of wealth between the bondholders and the stockholders but also the total value of the firm. Covenants can increase a firm's value (relative to value under a contract without covenants) by providing disincentives to, or restrictions on, exploitive stockholder behavior. For example, asset substitution incentives may be so powerful that under a contract without constraints stock- holders are willing to substitute an asset with a lower expected return so long as it has a sufficiently higher risk than the existing asset. Such a substitution increases stockholder wealth even though it decreases the firm's total value because the bondholders lose more than the stockholders' gain. Rational bondholders, however, anticipate that some of their claim will be expropriated through asset substitution and price their bonds accordingly (that is, they demand a higher rate).

Thus, in the absence of constraints on asset substitution, equilibriums involving debt financings have two features: First, firms will take more risks than in the presence of constraints (the incentive to substitute assets does not disappear just because the bondholders' anticipation of asset substitution is reflected in the interest rate). Second, a firm's stockholders will absorb the loss in the firm's value that results from the asset substitution.

Consequently, any covenant that restricts asset substitution (for example, a requirement to stay in the same business, a restriction on asset sales, or restrictions on investments, mergers, and acquisitions) can increase firm value. Because ultimately the stockholders gain from such restrictions in equilibrium, they will agree to covenants in debt contracts.

The theory of covenants and renegotiation emphasizes that covenants must be based on mutually observable and verifiable characteristics, actions, or events (see, for example, Berlin and Mester, 1992, and Huberman and Kahn, 1988).

Covenants cannot, for example, be written on characteristics, actions, or events that are observable only by the stockholders and not by the bondholders. Covenants also need to be observable and verifiable by third parties, such as a court of law. Characteristics, actions, or events that are observable but not verifiable cannot be included in covenants; however, they may still significantly affect an optimal debt contract. For example, a bank can refuse to renew a one-year loan on the basis of a mutually observable but non verifiable characteristic but would have difficulty legally declaring a two-year loan in default at the end of the first year because of a violation of a covenant written on that same characteristic. This example suggests that, in many cases, a short-term loan without a covenant may dominate a longer-term loan with a covenant (see Berlin, 1991, and Hart and Moore, 1989).

Although covenants can be written only on observable and verifiable characteristics, they may be related to non-verifiable and even unobservable characteristics. This relation greatly increases the power of covenants for mitigating bondholder- stockholder conflicts. A relation between observables and unobservable may exist for two reasons. First, observable, verifiable actions or events may be correlated with non-verifiable or unobservable actions or events. For example, the true risk of a firm, that is, the volatility of its returns, may not be observable. However, its current ratio may be correlated with this volatility and, therefore, serve as a proxy for risk. Second, an observable characteristic, action, or event may be related to an unobservable characteristic, action, or event through either self¬selection or incentive effects. For example, a firm's ability to take unobservable risks may be much greater in industry A than in industry B. Consequently, a covenant that restricts a firm to industry B limits the ability of a firm to alter its (unobservable) risk profile.

A financial covenant may have the same effect For example, a minimum current ratio requirement may constrain a borrower from selling on account to slow-paying customers. 81 Selling to such customers necessarily increases the observed liquidity risk of the firm because its current ratio deteriorates. It may also create an incentive to increase the firm's unobservable risk, to the extent that the firm has more ability to sell to unobservable (to the lender) riskier customers if it is permitted to extend trade credit on longer terms.

Collateral can also be used to mitigate bondholder-stockholder conflict. For example, a lien on firm assets (inside collateral) prevents borrowers from selling those assets without lender approval. 83 This limits the firm's ability to expropriate lender wealth through asset substitution (see Smith and Warner, 1979). Owners' pledging personal assets as collateral for a corporate loan (outside collateral) effectively increases their equity exposure. Such increased exposure may have important incentive effects depending on the owner's level of risk aversion. Outside collateral may also be useful in solving adverse selection problems because a borrowing firm's willingness to pledge collateral may reveal its true quality (see Chan and Kanatas, 1985), or it may be useful in solving incentive problems because it may alter the marginal return to risk shifting (that is, asset substitution) (see Boot, Thakor and Udell, 1991).

Theories of Financial Intermediation Information-based

Some theories of financial intermediation focus on the information problems associated with financial contracting. Such theories emphasize that financial intermediaries enjoy economies of scale in producing information about borrower quality because of fixed costs of producing information about any given borrower. Fixed costs make having only one or a few lenders for each borrower economical. Many small individual investors can delegate information-production responsibility to a single large financial intermediary that alone bears the fixed costs.

Commercial banks and life insurance companies are financial intermediaries in the spirit of these models. Both types of institution collect funds from many relatively small investors. These investors (depositors or policyholders) delegate due diligence and monitoring responsibility to the intermediary.

The Covenant-Monitoring-Renegotiation Paradigm

The literature on covenants and that on financial intermediation offer considerable insight into the ways in which markets address issues of bondholder-stockholder conflict. Separately, however, they fall short of describing the real- world financial landscape. The literature on covenants has not adequately addressed the association of covenant constraints with information production—due diligence at the origination stage and monitoring after loan funding. In addition, although covenant constraints can be value-enhancing to the extent that they minimize costs associated with borrower-stockholder conflict, they may also be value- reducing in that they may prevent the borrowing firm from investing in positive-value projects. A complete theory must account for the fact that borrowers choosing contracts with restrictive covenants also tend to be served by lenders that provide flexible renegotiation of the contracts. Borrowers agreeing to contracts with covenants want the option to pay off their loan or the ability to renegotiate the contract if they are constrained from investing in value-enhancing projects. Like loan origination, loan renegotiation requires that lenders produce information.

The existing information-based theories of financial intermediation fall short because they generally do not capture nor analyze the dynamic nature of intermediated loans: Intermediaries produce information both at thevorigination stage (lender due diligence) and on a more-or-less continuous basis after funding (monitoring). Dynamic production of information in conjunction with covenant restrictions enables a lender to declare a loan in default and demand immediate repayment if necessary while still offering flexibility through renegotiation. The information-based models also generally do not explain why some borrowers are served in intermediated markets and others in the public debt markets and why the contracts offered in those markets differ so dramatically. What has been missing in the theoretical literature until quite recently is a link between the theory of covenants, the mechanism of renegotiation, and the information-based theory of financial intermediation.

An initial attempt at a link was offered by Berlin and Mester (1992), who developed a theoretical model in which financial intermediaries extend loans that include restrictive covenants to borrowers. In their model, covenants are beneficial because they limit the problems discussed earlier.

Berlin and Mester's financial intermediaries use observable, but not necessarily verifiable, information to form the basis for renegotiation; renegotiation is beneficial because it enables borrowing firms to invest in positive-value projects that they otherwise would have forgone because of covenant restrictions.

In a more general setting than Berlin and Mester's, covenants can be viewed as a mechanism for triggering reevaluation of borrower riskiness by a financial intermediary. A covenant violation does not necessarily (and, indeed, usually does not) indicate that risk has increased. It can occur, for example, because a borrower wishes to invest in a new value-enhancing project that would trigger a violation of a covenant restricting new investments. Lenders can determine the appropriate response to a violation only if they analyze the borrower's situation, that is, if they produce information at the time of the violation. Simple monitoring during the life of the loan is often of little use except insofar as it improves the lender's ability to respond to covenant violations because, in the absence of a violation, lenders typically cannot change the terms of the loan no matter what their monitoring reveals.

Because financial intermediaries have a comparative advantage over small individual investors in producing information about borrower risk and in facilitating renegotiation, loans with covenants, especially financial covenants, are in general naturally made by intermediaries. Also, intermediaries may have more incentive to consider granting a covenant waiver than individual investors, as individual investors that do not expect to make many loans regularly in the future may perceive that they have little to gain from granting a waiver, whereas intermediaries that regularly invest in the market may profit from a reputation for being constructively flexible. Such a reputation may give intermediaries another competitive advantage over individual investors in conducting information¬ intensive lending.

This view of financial intermediation is our covenant-monitoring-renegotiation (CMR) paradigm. In the paradigm, information-intensive financial intermediaries serve information- problematic borrowers, not so much because they can more efficiently produce information at the origination stage but because they can efficiently employ covenants to control bondholder- stockholder conflicts. In equilibrium, lenders entering into debt contracts that include covenants must be able to monitor efficiently, that is, must efficiently produce information throughout the life of the contract. Lenders monitor a borrower's performance for two reasons: to determine whether the borrower is in compliance with covenants and to determine the proper action in the event of a violation. A covenant violation may indicate that the firm is in distress or signal that a borrower is taking actions not in the lender's interest. Covenant violations are a noisy signal about a borrower's prospects, however, because they can be based only on observable, verifiable information. To decide whether to liquidate a loan that is in technical default, to renegotiate its terms, or to waive the covenant, a lender must produce new information (including information that may not be verifiable) about the borrower, quite apart from simply determining whether the firm is in compliance with its covenants. This type of information production is often similar to that which occurs during loan origination.

Berlin and Mester (1992) demonstrate theoretically that the combination of tight covenants and the option to renegotiate becomes more valuable as a borrower's observable quality declines. The intuition behind this result is straightforward. For low-quality firms, information-related problems are more acute. Therefore, low-quality firms benefit the most from the inclusion of restrictive covenants in debt contracts because these covenants provide a mechanism for credibly committing to abstain from behavior that exploits the firm's lenders. However, restrictive covenants have a high probability of being binding in the future. Hence, the option to renegotiate is very valuable, and the reputation of lenders very important.

Covenants may be pareto-improving in any debt contract because they can constrain borrower behavior. Covenants used in conjunction with a debt contract offered by a financial intermediary may be especially potent, for three reasons. First, fixed costs of information production are kept down. Second, renegotiations are most feasible and least costly when the number of lenders is small. Third, because a borrower is often at a bargaining disadvantage in the event of a violation, it will contract initially only with lenders with a reputation for fair dealing in renegotiations. With their long-term presence in the credit markets, intermediaries are most able to build and maintain such reputations. Tight covenants are not present in widely distributed debt because diffuse owners cannot efficiently produce information, renegotiate, or maintain reputations.

Private Placements in a Theory of Credit Market Specialization

The CMR paradigm illuminates the differences among the commercial bank loan market, the private placement market, and the public bond market. Because their liabilities have short terms, banks prefer to invest in short-term assets. Such a preference naturally leads them to specialize in (among other things) lending to quite information- problematic, generally small firms. The optimal contract for such borrowers has a short maturity because renewal can be based on non- verifiable information. It still includes tight covenants because the borrowers are so problematic. These are frequently violated for reasons not associated with increases in expected losses or risk, and so bank loans tend to be renegotiated frequently.

Quite problematic borrowers accept restrictive terms because banks maintain a reputation for fair dealing and flexibility in renegotiation, because the covenant constraints have short terms, and because bank loans can typically be prepaid without penalty.

Because their liabilities have long terms, life insurance companies prefer to invest in long-term assets such as private placements, with fixed interest rates and call protection. Since the renewal-refusal mechanism for controlling risk is absent in such loans, life insurance companies rely more than banks on their ability to demand payment based on covenant violations, that is, on verifiable events. However, covenants are also less effective as a risk-control mechanism in long-term debt. Thus, in equilibrium, issuers of private placements tend to be less problematic, and covenants in private placements tend to be looser than in bank loans. As a result, private placement covenants are less frequently violated and renegotiated. With less frequent renegotiation, borrowers are more willing to rely on a lender's reputation for fair dealing, rather than on an ability to prepay without penalty if renegotiations go sour. Since reputation is important, the equilibrium can work only if private placements are fairly illiquid so that borrowers are assured of continued dealings with good lenders. Thus, the public bond market is not well suited to information-intensive lending. Although renegotiation occurs less frequently than in bank loans, not uncommonly a private placement is renegotiated several times during its life span. Life insurance companies invest significant resources in monitoring capacity (although not so many as banks do).

Public market borrowers pose relatively few information problems for lenders. Thus, publicly issued bonds can have long terms, and a relatively few, loose covenants are adequate. Intensive monitoring is unnecessary, and renegotiation is infrequent. Given these characteristics, ownership of public debt can be diffuse rather than concentrated, and the contracts can be liquid.

The CMR paradigm is not inconsistent with the traditional view of market segmentation, which focuses on transactions costs and regulation in explaining the institutional structure of credit markets. The traditional view is simply incomplete. In a sense, the traditional view emphasizes the liability side of bank and life insurance company balance sheets and largely ignores the asset side. The CMR paradigm focuses on the asset side. Consistent with the traditional view, the CMR paradigm indicates that long-term (short- term) loans appeal to life insurance companies (banks) because they match the maturity of their liabilities. However, it emphasizes that in equilibrium long-term and short¬term lenders will tend to serve different classes of borrowers and to use somewhat different risk-control technologies.

Other Empirical Evidence Relevant to the Theory of Credit Market Specialization

The CMR paradigm is consistent with empirical evidence indicating that financial intermediaries act as specialists in information production. James (1987) found a positive stock-price response to the announcement of bank credit agreements. This result is consistent with the notion that banks produce information about firm quality and reveal this information through their credit decisions (an approved bank credit agreement is a positive signal to the market); it contrasts with the results of numerous studies documenting a negative stock-price reaction to the issuance of public securities. One study subsequent to James (1987) indicates that the positive stock price response is confined to renewals (Lummer and McConnell, 1989), but another finds an effect for both new and renewed loans (Billet, Flannery, and Garfinkel, 1993). Wansley, Elayan, and Collins (1991) find that the availability of other signals of firm quality is important All of these studies conclude that the uniqueness of bank loans stems from the ability of banks, as financial intermediaries, to produce information not otherwise available in the market. Bailey and Mullineaux (1989) and Szewczyk and Varma (1991) document a similar positive stock- price response to the announcement of a private placement arrangement, suggesting that life insurance companies perform the same type of information production that commercial banks do.

Also consistent with the CMR paradigm is evidence that banks may have an advantage over insurance companies in the production of information about their borrowers. Besides helping to explain banks' preference for short¬term lending, such evidence helps explain why banks lend to a more problematic group of borrowers. Nakamura (1993), for example, argues that banks have a special advantage over other financial intermediaries because they obtain information from borrowers' checking accounts. This information is valuable because patterns in checking account activity can signal changes in a firm's quality.

Udell (1986) and Allen, Saunders, and Udell (1991) show theoretically and empirically that banks can sort borrowers by manipulating the prices of their multiple services, including demand deposits and loans. The more intensive information production by banks may also explain the contradiction between results found by Bailey and Mullineaux (1989) and Szewczyk and Varma (1991), which show a positive stock response to private placement, and other studies. James (1987) and Banning and James (1989) found a negative response, mostly associated with private placements that were used to repay bank debt Vora (1991) found a positive response but only for unrated firms.

The CMR paradigm is consistent with empirical evidence on corporate restructuring and bankruptcy.

Gilson, John, and Lang (1990) found that the probability that a firm would be restructured privately (versus entering formal bankruptcy) was positively related to the ratio of private debt (bank loans plus private placements) to total debt.

They also found that stock returns (that is, cumulative abnormal stock returns) were significantly higher on average for announcements of private restructurings (for which the returns were positive) than for bankruptcy (for which the returns were negative). One explanation for these results is that, in a private restructuring, firms avoid the direct and indirect costs associated with bankruptcy, which may total as much as 20 percent of firm value (see Warner, 1977, and Weiss, 1990, on direct costs; and Altman, 1984, Cutler and Summers, 1988, and Lang and Stultz, 1991, for indirect costs). As noted earlier, one advantage to intermediated debt is that it facilitates renegotiation. Hence, lower- quality firms with a higher probability of future distress value the renegotiation mechanism offered by financial intermediaries more than do higher-quality firms. Other things being equal, such firms will thus prefer to issue private rather than public debt. Another explanation for the higher cumulative stock returns associated with private restructurings is the possibility that relatively higher-quality firms signal their value by choosing to restructure privately.

Gilson, John, and Lang (1990) also examined stock returns at the time that the market first learned that a firm was in financial distress. They found that those firms subsequently entering bankruptcy proceedings suffered negative cumulative returns on average when the market first learned of their financial distress, whereas those firms subsequently restructured privately suffered no negative cumulative returns.

Taken together, the Gilson, John, and Lang results are generally consistent with the CMR paradigm. Financial intermediaries can use information produced through borrower monitoring in conjunction with restrictive covenants to begin negotiations leading to a restructuring before a firm deteriorates beyond a point of no return. That is, financial intermediaries may be able to intervene at the earlier stages of firm distress because of three characteristics of intermediated debt contracts: covenant restrictions, monitoring by lenders, and the flexibility in renegotiation that is associated with a limited number of lenders.

Therefore, among those firms that suffer distress, those with intermediated debt are more likely to restructure privately. Firms without intermediated debt, however, are likely to suffer more deterioration before negotiations begin and are more likely to enter bankruptcy. This finding is also consistent with the results of Franks and Torous (1990), who found that firms filing for bankruptcy are generally in poorer condition than those restructuring privately. In particular, bankrupt firms are less liquid and less solvent than those that work out their debt in private restructurings.

CHAPTER 4

Secondary Trading, the New Market for Rule 144A Private Placements, and the Role of Agents.

In focusing on an economic analysis of the traditional market for privately placed debt, we ignored two important features of that market: the effects of Rule 144A and the role of agents.

Though resale of private placements is some- times thought to be prohibited, in fact a small secondary market for them has existed for decades. Rule 144A, however, has created a new market for private placements. Adopted in April 1990 by the SEC, this rule establishes conditions under which private placements may be freely traded among certain classes of institutional investors. The rule has spawned the development of a market for underwritten private placements, which has characteristics—such as not being information intensive—more like those of the public bond market than like those of the traditional private market. We earlier, analyzes the Rule 144A market.

The great majority of new private issues are assisted by an agent, which offers many of the advisory and distribution services of a public bond underwriter but does not actually perform a firm-commitment underwriting, except with underwritten Rule 144A issues. Agents are at the nexus of many private market information flows and thus play an important role. Here we describe their role also.

1. The Rule 144A Market

Rule 144A gave securities firms the opportunity to underwrite private placements, allowing new issues of private debt to be distributed in much the same way as issues in the public bond market.

Securities firms have taken advantage of this opportunity by providing public-like borrowers an alternative to the public market and the traditional private placement market. The 144A market thus bridges a gap between the two existing markets by making available to large corporations, not having the information problems of the typical issuer of private debt, a more efficient means of placing debt in the private market.

Although Rule 144A applies only to certain secondary market transactions, it has implications for the distribution of private placements. The rule permits sophisticated financial institutions, designated in the rule as qualified institutional buyers (QIBs), to trade private placements freely among themselves without jeopardizing the exemption of the securities from SEC registration. In any private placement transaction, whether in the primary or in the secondary market, the seller must ensure that the sale does not constitute a public offering, which would violate the basis for exemption.

Before the adoption of Rule 144A, securities firms did not underwrite private placements because sales of securities to investors as part of an underwritten distribution might be construed as a public offering. Rule 144A, however, takes the view that QIBs are not part of the public; consequently, transactions between QIBs cannot involve a public distribution. Most securities firms are QIBs, and thus they can purchase private placements from issuers and resell them to other QIBs without violating the private placement exemption.

The SEC justified this treatment of QIBs on the grounds that the Congress had never considered sophisticated, institutional investors to need the protection offered by the registration of securities. The purpose of registration was to protect unsophisticated, individual investors. The SEC there- fore concluded that, if secondary transactions involved only sophisticated investors, such transactions would not constitute a public distribution and thus could be affected without restriction.

The SEC had two basic purposes in adopting Rule 144A. One was to increase liquidity in the private placement market and thus to lower the differential between private and public yields. The other was to make the private placement market more attractive to foreign issuers. Foreign companies had been infrequent issuers in the public markets, primarily because they found the registration requirements expensive and burdensome, especially the stipulation that financial statements be reconciled with generally accepted accounting principles in the United States. 103 Although foreign companies have long been able to bypass these obstacles by issuing private placements, they had not done so to any great extent, partly because of the higher yields in the private market than those in the public market. The negotiation of terms and frequent inclusion of restrictive covenants in private debt contracts also made the private placement market unattractive to foreign companies.

As defined in Rule 144A, QIBs are financial institutions, corporations, and partnerships that own and invest on a discretionary basis at least $100 million in securities. 104 This definition is broad enough to include life insurance companies, pension funds, investment companies, foreign and domestic commercial banks, master and collective bank trusts, and savings and loan associations.

Besides meeting the securities test, banks and savings and loans must have net worth of at least $25 million. The SEC imposed this condition because it believed that securities holdings alone did not necessarily reflect the appropriate degree of investor sophistication for institutions having insured deposits. 105 In contrast to other institutional investors, a broker-dealer must own only $10 million in securities to qualify as a QIB. The SEC chose a lower amount to avoid excluding a significant number of brokers-dealers that were actively participating in the private placement market.

Besides confining transactions to QIBs, Rule 144A stipulates three other conditions. First, to ensure that a minimum amount of information is available, an issuer must provide buyers with copies of its recent financial statements and basic information about its business. Second, when issued, privately placed securities cannot be of the same class as any of the issuer's securities already traded on a U.S. stock exchange or on the NASDAQ system. This requirement is intended to prevent the development of an institutional market in publicly traded securities. Third, the seller of 144A securities must take "reasonable" steps to inform the buyer that the sale is occurring pursuant to Rule 144A,

Features of the Market

Although the SEC adopted Rule 144A only in 1990, the 144A market has developed so that it is easily distinguished from the traditional private placement market. In our view, the essential feature of the new market is that it is not information intensive, which is to say that it has taken on the main features of the public bond market. The most visible and discussed similarity to the public market has been the underwriting of 144A offerings. Indeed, this aspect serves as the basis for our definitions of a 144A security and the 144A market.

Nature and Size

Measuring the development of the underwritten 144A market is especially difficult because many market participants, as well as the information services that collect data on the private placement market, consider a 144A security to be any private placement that relies upon the documentation required for a financing pursuant to Rule 144A. Unfortunately, this definition includes private placements that are, other than the documentation, no different from traditional private placements.

Thus, relying upon these data, for which we have no alternative, necessarily leads to an overstatement of the size of the underwritten 144A market.

Using the broad definition, gross issuance of 144A securities has expanded rapidly since the inception of the 144A market in 1990. The volume of offerings in 1992 was about $33 billion, almost double that in 1991 (the first full year the rule was in effect) and nearly two- thirds of the volume in the traditional market.

The difficult question to answer is, how much of the broad measure of 144A issuance has been underwritten? No direct estimates have been made, but an indirect estimate of underwritten issuance can be obtained by assuming that issues with two or more credit ratings have been underwritten. Underwritten offerings, whether in the public market or the 144A market, typically have at least two ratings because the underwriters otherwise incur significantly higher regulatory capital charges. Available information from the SEC shows $4.4 billion of 144A issues with at least two ratings in 1991 and $6.0 billion in the first eleven months of 1992. These figures are roughly in line with market estimates, which place underwritten issuance in 1991 at slightly more than $3 billion and in the first half of 1992 at roughly double that pace. Even the larger figures from the SEC suggest that the underwritten market is still in an early stage of development.

Characteristics of Underwritten 144A Securities

Besides being underwritten, 144A securities have assumed many other features of publicly offered bonds. The terms and documents generally conform to the standards used in the public market; in particular, bonds have "public style" covenants, which are fewer and considerably less restrictive than those found in traditional private placements. Underwriters charge roughly the same fees as those for a public offering, but the issuer avoids the considerable expenses associated with public registration. The underwritten 144A securities also generally have two credit ratings; and, in many instances, the offering memorandum is styled like a prospectus in a public offering. Also, 144A offerings are usually transferred through the book-entry system operated by the Depository Trust

Company. All of these features are a part of underwriters' efforts to market 144A private placements to traditional public market investors, such as mutual funds, pension funds, and groups within life insurance companies responsible for public bond investments. Furthermore, under- written private placements have been comparable in size more to public offerings than to traditional private placements: In 1991, for example, the average issue for 144A securities, broadly defined, was $92 million, nearly double that for non-144A placements. Finally, the terms of the securities are rarely negotiated with investors but are typically set before the offering.

Despite this similarity to public bonds, under- written 144A securities generally have not yet achieved the same degree of liquidity as public bonds, and thus their yields contain a premium. In the first year of the market, the premium was reported to be about the same as that on traditional private placements. More recent reports suggest, however, that the liquidity of 144A securities has increased and that the premium has decreased, as major dealers have allocated capital and traders to making markets for 144A securities.

Foreign Issuers

Thus far, the proportion of foreign issuance has been greater in the 144A market than in either the traditional private or the public bond market. Based upon the broad measure of 144A issuance, approximately one-third of the total volume of 144A offerings in 1991 and 1992 was accounted for by foreign issuers, including U.S. subsidiaries of foreign companies. In contrast, 17 percent of the traditional private placements and 6 percent of the public offerings were by foreign issuers.

Several factors lie behind foreign use of the 144A market. One is that the adoption of Rule 144A itself served to publicize the already existing advantages of the private placement market to foreign companies. Thus, the effect of the rule has been to alter foreigners' perception that all offerings in the United States are subject to excessive regulatory burdens. Indeed, market participants concede that some of the foreign issuance done under Rule 144A could have been as easily accomplished before the rule's adoption. Moreover, since the rule's adoption, investment banks have devoted greater effort to bringing foreign issuers to the private placement market. A second factor boosting foreign issuance has been the low interest rates in the United States relative to those in European countries. The increase in 1991 in foreign issuance in the public bond market and the record pace of offerings in 1992 attest to the yield advantage in U.S. markets. A final factor is that the premium in yields on foreign bonds issued in the private placement market has declined.

Among other aspects of foreign issuance in the 144A market, many foreign issuers have been well-known corporations, but at the same time, about 20 percent of the issues have come from first-time borrowers in the United States. The major sources of issuance from abroad have been the United Kingdom and Mexico.

Through November 1992, more than half of the foreign issues studied by the SEC were involved in global offerings, and virtually all the global offerings originated with an offshore entity. In contrast, about half of those foreign-related offerings confined solely to the 144A market involved U.S. subsidiaries of foreign corporations. About 50 percent of the volume of foreign 144A securities in 1991-92 came from financial institutions, and most of that was in medium-term notes.

Domestic Issuers

Despite the attention given to foreign use of the 144A market, U.S. companies have accounted for nearly 70 percent of the volume through 1992.

Domestic issuers in the 144A market have typically been those companies with special circumstances that preclude issuing in the public bond market, where yields are lower. In some cases, the companies have not wanted to spend the time nor incur the expense required to register the securities with the SEC. Among these have been private companies that, in the past, have borrowed in the traditional market but have now found more favorable pricing in the 144A market. Also included are nonregistered subsidiaries of publicly registered parents that have issued debt in the subsidiaries' names. In other cases, companies with outstanding public securities have turned to the underwritten 144A market to protect the confidentiality of the specific circumstances leading to the borrowing.

Another group of domestic companies has used the 144A market as a temporary alternative to the public bond market. These companies normally issue public securities but have turned to the 144A market to avoid any delays arising during the registration process that could cause issuers to miss favorable financing opportunities. The 144A private placements sold under these circumstances have included registration rights, which obligate the issuer to register the bonds with the SEC within a specified time. Failure to do so results in the bonds' carrying higher coupon rates. Most companies selling these types of 144A securities have been rated below investment grade.

Investors

During the first two years after the adoption of Rule 144A, life insurance companies were the largest group of investors in 144A securities. As the 144A market has developed features of the public bond market, however, the composition of investors has shifted toward those, such as mutual funds and pension funds, that generally concentrate investments in public securities.

Information on buyers of 144A securities from a sample of new issues studied by the SEC implies that the share of life insurers' purchases of straight debt fell from roughly 75 percent between April 1990 and August 1991 to 60 percent between September 1991 and April 1992   (SEC, 1993). Over the same two periods, the combined share of mutual funds and pension funds rose from a little over 10 percent to nearly 40 percent. Market participants indicate that the composition of buyers has continued to shift toward mutual funds and pension funds and, in addition, that many life insurances companies have shifted responsibility for investing in 144A securities from their private placement groups to their public market groups. Thus, the dominance of the life insurance companies in the later period of the SEC study likely understates the growing significance of public market investors in the 144A market.

Public market investors are attracted to the 144A market because its public-like features suit their investment style. In contrast to the buy-and- hold strategy of investors in traditional private placements, many public market investors follow a total-return strategy in which they attempt to increase the return beyond the security's coupon rate of interest. To do so, these investors look for undervalued securities offering the potential for capital gains. Such investors require liquidity, because they do not expect to hold the securities to maturity. From this perspective, public market investors have found the liquidity in the 144A market to be sufficient.

In contrast to the move of public market investors to the 144A market, buyers of traditional private placements are unlikely over time to find this market attractive. The comparative advantage of traditional market investors is in credit analysis and credit monitoring, neither of which is required extensively in the 144A and public markets. And, in the buy-and-hold strategy of traditional investors, liquidity is of little importance.

Prospects for Development

Because it has filled a gap in U.S. capital markets, the underwritten 144A market appears likely to undergo further development and growth. Before the adoption of Rule 144A, no market existed that could accommodate large issues that were unsuited for the public market but did not require an information-intensive market. Issuers of this nature, whether domestic or foreign, had no choice in U.S. markets but to accept the terms of the private market. Although such issuers often did not have to tolerate restrictive covenants, they had to pay a premium over public bond rates because of the lack of liquidity in the private placement market. By increasing liquidity, Rule 144A has reduced the premium and has thus increased offerings by such issuers.

In being both non-information-intensive and private, the 144A market represents a new bond market Whether the need for such a market extends much beyond current levels of activity is an open question. The midsized, information- problematic firms, which issue in the traditional market, will probably not move to the 144A market. They must borrow from a financial intermediary and often do not want their issues to be traded in a liquid market to investors that might not understand their particular circumstances.

Perhaps, the greatest potential for the 144A market lies in its use by foreign issuers, inasmuch as they represent the largest group of borrowers with no previous satisfactory alternative in the United States. If foreign issuance expands significantly, Rule 144A may prove helpful in integrating world capital markets. Borrowing by large, domestic corporations with specialized requirements seems to offer much less potential, as such borrowing constitutes a small share of the credit needs of large corporations. If, however, the liquidity of the 144A market increases so that yields in the public and 144A markets are roughly the same, a considerable portion of public market borrowing may shift to the 144A market, which would offer lower borrowing costs overall because of the absence of registration costs.

The Role of Agents

Almost all new public issues of bonds are managed by an underwriter on the basis of a firm commitment. New issues of private placements, however, are often assisted by an agent or adviser. Agents provide various services to issuers, including advice about the structure, pricing, and timing of financings; assistance in locating investors; and help in negotiating with them. Agents assist traditional private issues on a best-efforts basis, but many Rule 144A transactions are firm commitment underwritings.

Although no quantitative evidence is available, remarks by market participants indicate that an agent assists in about two-thirds of traditional private issues; the rest of these issues involve direct contacts between issuers and investors. Apparently, although lenders and borrowers in the private placement market might be able to find each other and write contracts by themselves, such a process would be costly; in many cases, employment of a third-party agent is more efficient.

The role of agents in the private placement market is somewhat more complicated than the previous paragraph may imply. Like the private market itself, the agent industry exists primarily to solve problems associated with costly and asymmetric information. Agents add value in several ways:

- They reduce search costs for both borrowers and lenders by maintaining information about lenders' preferences and by screening out unqualified borrowers.
- They have knowledge of prevailing market prices and the tradeoff rates between prices and other contract terms. Borrowers need such information for both search and negotiation, and buying it from an agent is often cheaper than gathering it.
- They provide technical advice and other assistance to borrowers during negotiations, helping them obtain better terms.
- They enforce informal bargaining conventions that reduce bargaining costs for everyone.

The private market is thus broader and deeper than it would be without agents: More borrowers are served, and more competition exists among lenders.

The structure of the agent industry is influenced by economies of scale and scope, by limited strategic relationships between agents and lenders, and to some extent by specialization. The primary economy of scope is with the provision of other corporate financial services: Agents tend to flourish in those large commercial banks and investment banks that sell a large volume and variety of corporate finance products, such as loans or underwritings. The relationship officers of such banks can refer significant numbers of potential clients to the private placement agents within the organization. Economies of scope also exist with public- issue underwriting, in that sales forces for public securities can distribute some private placements.

The primary economy of scale is related to the costs of gathering information. These costs are smaller for high- volume agents for two reasons. First, the fixed costs of gathering information can be spread over many clients. Second, an agent acquires information as a byproduct of assisting individual transactions, both reducing the amount of information it must gather by other means and providing more to trade in the information marketplace. Agents and lenders gather information through informal sharing arrangements with each other, and high-volume participants are more sought after as partners in such arrangements.

Economies of scale and scope influence an agent's style of providing services as well as the degree of concentration of the industry. Although most agents are in large measure generalists, they have some variety in the technologies they can choose when conducting their business, especially with regard to the distribution of securities. They also tend to specialize somewhat in the technologies best suited to the kinds of client their host organization's relationship officers tend to refer.

Although large agents may have advantages, competition appears substantial because entry and exit costs are relatively low and the roster of agents is constantly changing.

Who Are the Agents?

According to a database supplied by the publishers of the Investment Dealers' Digest, thirty investment banks and commercial banks were responsible for 96 percent of the volume of all agented privately placed debt transactions from 1989 through 1991 (see table 10). Each of these agents placed at least $1 billion of debt securities during at least one of those three years. The database, however, does not include all new private issues. Possibly, a table based on a complete list of transactions would change the ranking somewhat and would add entries to the list.

The Private Placement Transaction Stages

This subsection describes the role of the agent at each stage of private placement issuance, emphasizing the ways in which agents add economic value to the transaction. Readers not already familiar with the details of private issuance may find the description of a sample private placement transaction that appears in appendix F helpful at this point. The example provides a sense of the flow of the process that may be useful background for the analysis in this section.

As shown in the following diagram, a deal passes through five major stages. During the prospecting stage, agents identify potential issuers and compete with each other to gain the issuer's business. Issuers decide whether to place a private issue or to use another vehicle for financing and whether to hire an agent or to issue without assistance.

During the contract design stage, and sometimes during prospecting, agents analyze in detail an issuer's condition, operations, and plans (due diligence) and use this information to set major debt contract terms. They summarize the terms on a term sheet and write an offering memorandum describing the issuer, which is somewhat similar to a prospectus. The memorandum and term sheet are often packaged together and called "the book." If necessary, agents seek a rating of the issue. They then choose an initial strategy for distribution and, in some cases, carry out preliminary inquiries of investors.

During the distribution stage, which is coincident with the design stage for many deals, the agent seeks investors. Negotiations that change the term sheet often occur. In some cases, the agent first seeks a lead lender (traditionally, the investor that buys the largest fraction of the placement) and conducts most negotiations with it; only after the lead has committed to the deal does the agent attempt a broader distribution. In other cases, the agent attempts a broad distribution from the beginning. An initial commitment by a lender is known as "circling" the deal. Such a commitment is contingent on approval by the lender's investment committee and on due diligence by the lender that produces satisfactory verification of the information in the offering memorandum. Negotiations about price are conducted in terms of spreads over Treasuries of comparable average life until a deal is fully subscribed, at which time coupon rates are set. If necessary, to attract additional investors, the coupon rate may be increased after it has been set, but it may not be reduced even if Treasury rates fall between rate-setting and closing. Similarly, if Treasury rates rise, by tradition the lenders may not demand a higher coupon.

The contract design and distribution stages typically require one to two months. The process of obtaining a rating is the most important source of delays.

The penultimate stage, due diligence by lenders, begins when a deal is fully subscribed. Before circling, lenders carry out a significant amount of credit analysis, which often involves gathering some information not found in the offering memorandum. During the due diligence stage, lenders verify the information in the offering memorandum and, if satisfied, present the deal to investment committees for approval. Rarely do investment committees reject a deal for anything but unsatisfactory due diligence. Rejection after circling imposes large costs on other members of the lending syndicate and on agents and borrowers. Agents are less likely to bring deals to a lender with a history of such behavior, and other lenders are less willing to join it in syndicates.

Rejections thus in the long run affect a lender's ability to invest in private placements on favorable terms. In the final stage of private issuance, lawyers hammer out the language of the debt contract, which involves several documents besides the notes themselves. The lenders are represented by a bond counsel, which is by tradition chosen by the lead lender but paid by the borrower. The borrower is often represented by its own counsel and is usually assisted by the agent. Transactions can unravel at this point when interpretations of term sheets differ, but such unraveling is relatively rare. Although it varies, the time required for the final stage is usually a few weeks. Once all parties sign the contract (closing), funds can be disbursed to the borrower.

The remainder of this subsection describes and analyzes each of the stages in more detail.

Prospecting, Initial Advice, and Inter-Agent Competition

Commercial banks and investment banks obtain most of their private placement clients through contacts initiated by relationship officers, who are traditional bank loan officers, investment bankers responsible primarily for maintaining relationships with clients, and hybrids of the two. Relationship officers call on current or prospective clients of their organization, attempt to learn about the broad spectrum of client needs for capital and financial services, and in the process often help clients to recognize opportunities and incipient problems.

These officers are also able to identify opportunities to sell specific products.

Relationship officers consult their private placement group when they recognize that a private placement may be an appropriate way for a client to raise funds. When several different borrowing strategies might serve a client's interests, some organizations arrange presentations to the client by different groups within the organization, for example, the private placement group and the loan syndication group.

The prospecting process sometimes departs from this description at some commercial banks where most customer contact is by traditional loan officers and where the loan officers' compensation is determined by success in originating loans. This type of compensation scheme may deter loan officers from recommending a private placement over a commercial loan. According to market participants, commercial banks are losing this weakness as they change their organizational structures and compensation schemes.

Agents may also obtain clients through requests by previous private placement clients for help with new transactions. Such requests are sometimes made directly to the agent group, as the client already knows them. Direct requests are also received from potential issuers who want competitive bids from different agents. Relatively few agenting jobs for first-time clients result from prospecting by the private placement group itself.

Agents compete for the right to assist particular private placements, with the degree of competition depending both on expected profits and on the extent to which a borrower seeks multiple bids.

Some agents specialize in particular types of transactions, and thus their explicit costs and opportunity costs differ across transaction types, so a given borrower can be quoted a variety of fees. Competition exists also along dimensions other than fees, as borrowers must estimate both the likelihood that a given agent can successfully distribute the securities and the interest rate and other loan terms that the agent can obtain. Borrowers do not typically possess the information required to make such estimates with precision, so they must rely, at least to some extent, on reputations and on the claims made by agents in sales presentations. Agents from an organization with which a borrower has a satisfactory, ongoing relationship thus have a significant advantage in competing for that borrower's private placement business.

Value Added. A considerable amount of economic value is added by agents during the prospecting, advice, and competition stage of a transaction. Some borrowers know little or nothing about the private market and may not consider it as a source of funds unless it is suggested by a relationship officer. Even if they are somewhat informed, borrowers will usually not commit to bear the opportunity costs associated with a private market offering without first comparing the opportunities there with those in other markets. Such a comparison can be done only with reasonably current and complete information about the operation of the private market and the terms available there. The costs of gathering such information are much higher for the private placement market than for the bank loan and public debt markets, especially if the borrower has never issued a private placement. Either directly or through their organization's relationship officers, agents provide such information to potential borrowers as part of their marketing efforts and thus improve the efficiency of financial markets.

Economies of Scale and Scope. Although avail- able data do not support precise measurement, the remarks of market participants imply that economies of scale and scope at the prospecting, advice, and inter-agent competition stage of transactions strongly influence the structure of the market for agent services. An agent organization need not be large, but it must bear the staff and overhead costs of near-continuous gathering of information about private market conditions and of maintaining relations with lenders. Thus, the number of relationship officers calling on clients likely to issue private placements must be sufficient to yield clients paying fees that at least cover costs.

Although the organization as a whole is not absolutely required to be large, commercial banks and investment banks that serve many corporate clients of medium to large size are more likely to provide a large flow of private placement prospects to their agent groups. Such organizations can thus spread the overhead costs of information gathering over a broader base of revenues. In other words, scope economies may exist between agenting and providing other financial services to medium and large corporations. Commercial banks that focus mainly on small business lending, mortgage loans, or consumer lending will have difficulty making a profit on private placement agenting.

Indirect evidence of economies of scope can be seen in the rankings of the thirty major agents according to their volume of commercial banking and investment banking business. Bank holding companies were ranked by the total consolidated volume of commercial and industrial loans on their books at the end of 1991. 126 Investment banks were ranked according to the total volume of domestic securities issues of all kinds for which they acted as lead manager.

As with the ranking of agents, we claim not that the order of rankings is entirely accurate or important but only that a significant ranking indicates a large volume of activity in the capital markets.

The top twenty-six agents rank among the top twenty commercial banks or the top fifteen investment banks, or both. All of the top fifteen investment banks are major agents, as are all of the top five commercial banks. Fifteen of the top twenty commercial banks reportedly acted as agent at least once. This predominance of large commercial and investment banks in the agenting industry is consistent with the existence of significant economies of scale and scope in agenting.

The economies of scale and scope realized at the prospecting, advice, and competition stage influence an agent's strategy and specialization. An agent within a commercial or investment bank that serves mainly Fortune 500 and large international corporations will naturally find most of its clients coming from those groups. As is discussed further below, design and distribution of the private issues of such borrowers is typically different from that for middle-market borrowers, and it is efficient for the agent to gather somewhat different information and to maintain somewhat different relationships with lenders than an agent specializing in serving middle-market borrowers.

Design of Major Contract Terms and Distribution of Securities

Having won an issuer's business, an agent begins designing and perhaps distributing the securities. Design involves setting the terms of the securities, including payment amounts, timing, and covenants. Distribution involves finding lenders that will buy the securities. In contrast to the phases of public issuance, the line between the design and distribution phases is blurred and, in some cases, does not exist because design of the terms of privately placed securities often involves negotiations between lenders and borrowers. The negotiations may be implicit or explicit and may take place either before or during the period when the securities are offered to lenders. The nature and the timing of the negotiations depend to a large extent on the style of distribution chosen by the agent, which in turn depends on the identity of the agent, the characteristics of the borrower and the loan, and market conditions.

At one extreme, the process can resemble a best-efforts public underwriting. Here the agent uses its knowledge of market conditions and lenders' preferences to design terms that are likely to satisfy lenders, including an interest rate spread. The securities are then offered to many potential investors on a take-it-or-leave-it basis. If the issue cannot be fully sold, the interest rate may be increased or other terms may be changed. There is often no lead lender in the usual sense, although one lender may be designated as lead.

At the other extreme, the agent may contact one or a few potential lenders immediately upon receiving a mandate from the issuer and inform them of the identity of the borrower and the likely amount of the loan. Reactions of the lenders and ensuing negotiations influence the terms of the securities. By the time the term sheet is finalized, distribution may be pro forma because all or almost all of the lenders may have made informal commitments. Any unsold portion is made available to investors at large, although they have no opportunity to negotiate the terms.

Between these extremes is a continuum of styles. One part of the design phase, however, does not vary much across styles: due diligence. Due Diligence. Agents of traditional private placements do not bear the market price risks associated with public underwriting, as non¬underwritten placements never appear on agents' books. Agents are nevertheless at risk, in three ways. First, they are paid only for successful placements, and thus their investment in a particular transaction of staff time and other resources is at risk until closing. Deals can unravel for many reasons; one is a lender's discovery after circling but before formal commitment that the offering memorandum misrepresented the borrower's circumstances.

Second, the agent's reputation with lenders is at risk. Lenders also invest time and resources in evaluating potential loans, and the semiformal loan commitment that circling a deal represents is based mainly on the information in the offering memorandum and term sheet If in performing its own due diligence a lender finds an offer memo to be materially incomplete or inaccurate, it will be less likely in the future to expend resources in considering transactions proposed by that agent. Also, if an agent is associated with too many placements that later decline in credit quality or go into default, lenders will be less likely to deal with that agent.

Third, private placement agents have been named as parties in some lender-liability lawsuits. Agents must thus take the potential costs associated with such suits into account when estimating the profits from assisting a transaction.

Agent control these risks by conducting a close examination of a borrower's business, financial position, and plans. They perform this due diligence immediately after they receive a mandate to assist a borrower's placement and, to some extent, before that. This examination resembles the due diligence performed by lenders and usually includes a visit to the borrower's headquarters or other relevant sites. Besides controlling risks, the examination provides the agent with information needed to write the offer memo and term sheet.

Some commercial banks and investment banks are sufficiently concerned about these risks that private placement agenting jobs must be approved by a credit committee. Some market participants stated that their committees reject a substantial fraction of agenting jobs.

Value Added from Due Diligence by Agents.

Two ways in which agents add value are by Pre¬screening borrowers and by gathering information needed by potential lenders. Each of the large private market lenders is offered hundreds of placements in a typical year and refuses all but a small fraction. 130 At the typical large lender, an initial evaluation occurs when the agent offers the transaction. This evaluation is based mainly upon information in the offering memorandum and term sheet. Some proposed transactions can be quickly rejected, because they fail to meet the investor's credit criteria, its yield objective, or its diversification requirements. Others require more extensive evaluation, but this is still based on information in the offering memorandum and any additional information communicated during negotiations.

Lenders typically perform their own due diligence to verify the information in the offering memorandum only after circling a deal.

The typical placement is offered to many potential lenders. The process would be inefficient if each of them gathered all the information required either to reject or to circle a deal and if each had to weed out obviously unqualified borrowers. In such a situation, the aggregate staff costs associated with private placement lending would be much larger.

Agents improve the efficiency of the intermediation process by performing these two functions. To do so, they must perform due diligence similar to that done by lenders during the verification stage. As noted, such examinations of borrowers begin during the prospecting, advice, and interjacent competition stages. At this point, many potential borrowers that are not actually able to issue are weeded out on the basis of a modest amount of information-gathering and effort by the agent.

Resources are saved because only one organization processes and rejects the "applications" of such borrowers and because only one organization gathers the information that appears in the offering memorandum. This division of labor works because agents that do not perform adequate due diligence will quickly acquire a bad reputation. 133 Lenders do not actually commit funds based only on an agent's due diligence, but they are willing to incur the costs of initial evaluations. If they later find that the agent did not conduct a thorough evaluation or misrepresented the facts, they can prevent further losses by backing out of the deal. In the relatively small community of private placement professionals, the agent's reputation will be tarnished, not only with that lender but with other lenders as well. The agent will then be at a competitive disadvantage, as lenders will be less willing to consider placements offered by it in the future. Thus, the incentives of agents (with regard to due diligence) are kept closely enough in line with those of lenders that the efficiencies of having agents perform much of the pre¬screening can be captured.

Determinants of the Style of Design and Distribution. The terms of a private placement are determined mainly by market conditions and the risks associated with lending to the borrower. Securities issued by risky or information- problematic borrowers must include more covenants or a higher rate of interest or both. However, the process by which the terms are determined may influence the nature of the terms and the costs associated with issuance. The process includes the negotiating strategies adopted by the issuer and agent and the way in which lenders are identified.

For example, an agent may be uncertain whether or not lenders will insist on a covenant restricting a borrower's interest coverage ratio. If the agent makes preliminary inquiries, the lenders will know that such a covenant is negotiable and will be more likely to insist on it. The agent may offer securities without the covenant to lenders sequentially, hoping to find some that make counteroffers not including the covenant. But a sequential offering runs the risk that some lenders that would enter negotiations if they saw the covenant on the term sheet will reject the deal entirely. Returning to such lenders after completing the sequence is difficult. Also, sequential negotiations can be time-consuming and costly and in a long-run equilibrium agents' fees must reflect costs. Thus, competitive pressures often militate against sequential offerings. Instead, the agent may offer securities to many lenders simultaneously, on a first- come, first-served basis. If the issue is not fully subscribed, terms can be changed in response to lenders' counteroffers and another offering made. However, a simultaneous offering can be more expensive than a sequential offering that is quickly subscribed, as more lenders are involved. Also, for placements that require a lead lender, a simultaneous offering to the universe of lenders may be infeasible because smaller lenders will not consider some deals until a lead lender has circled.

In cooperation with the borrower, an agent makes decisions on four matters in determining the style of a distribution:

1. The terms included in the initial term sheet
2. The extent to which the initial terms will be represented as non-negotiable
3. Whether to seek a lead lender as the first step in distribution
4. The manner of solicitation of lenders (sequential or simultaneous) and the number and identity of those solicited.

Decisions are aimed at obtaining good terms while limiting the agent's costs of design and distribution. At the outset, the agent commits to assist the issuer for a fee equal to a fixed percentage of the loan, and thus the agent's profits are directly related to its costs. Agents usually avoid high-risk strategies because they collect fees only for successful distributions. They also consider the effects of a strategy on their reputations and relationships with lenders. Negotiating strategies that annoy lenders may hamper an agent's ability to do business in the future.

In this context, several factors appear to be the primary determinants of the decisions that are made. One is the complexity or severity of the information problems posed by the borrower's business, financial structure, and corporate structure and by the complexity of the financing in progress. Complexities force potential lenders to invest more resources in credit analysis and, in some cases, not all lenders will have the necessary expertise. There is an incentive to find a lead lender for such placements, as the agent can use the lead's commitment as a signal to other investors that necessary analyses have been done and that the terms are satisfactory. There is also an incentive to offer the placement initially to only one or to a few potential lead lenders, as they will be more likely to invest in the necessary analysis if they know that competition to buy the placement will be limited until the terms are set.

A second factor is the rating of the borrower and any prospective changes in its condition. Because default risk varies much more across B-rated borrowers than across A-rated borrowers, lenders must do much more analysis of lower- rated borrowers before they can negotiate terms. Here, again, an incentive exists to find a lead lender and to negotiate initially with only a few potential leads. Lenders, being also more reluctant to lend to borrowers that appear to be headed downhill, insist on more stringent covenants to control risk. They will be more likely to enter negotiations if the initial term sheet includes a strong covenant package, as it is a signal that the borrower recognizes the problem and will not impose unusually large negotiating costs on the lender over the term of the loan.

The distribution facilities available to the agent are a third factor affecting distribution strategy.

When a financing is highly rated and straightforward, requiring relatively little analysis by lenders, a lead lender may be unnecessary, and offering the placement simultaneously to the universe of buyers of private placements may be possible.

Some large investment banks use their fixed- income sales forces to make such offers. Because these sales forces already bear the fixed costs of staying in communication with a large group of buyers, this method can be cheaper to implement than distributions made solely by the less specialized members of the private placement group.

Thus, other things being equal, agents with such distribution channels at their disposal are more likely to offer a placement simultaneously to many buyers.

A widespread distribution may not always be feasible. Besides the reasons already given, if a borrower wants to maintain confidentiality about the transaction, the offering is likely to be shown to a limited number of lenders. Lenders can extract a premium from such borrowers, of course, as breaking off negotiations and turning to another potential lender are costly to the borrower. An inexperienced or uninformed agent is more likely to offer a placement to a few lenders at a time and solicit counteroffers from them than to offer to several lenders on a take-it-or-leave-it basis. Such an agent may lack the knowledge required to choose an optimal set of terms and may also have relationships with only a few lenders. A distribution may also be limited if a borrower wishes to establish a relationship with a particular set of investors. Finally, although in principle a broad distribution by a fixed-income sales force may be done quickly for some standard placement, in cases where rapid progress on negotiations and approvals is required the number of lenders often must be small.

Market conditions, too, may influence distribution strategies. When demand is high for placements in general or for particular kinds of placements, agents are more likely to write initial term sheets with fewer and looser covenants and to suggest rates slightly below market.

This framework is a basis for describing the spectrum of placement design and distribution styles already mentioned. Agents are most likely to choose a style similar to a best-efforts public underwriting (involving an offering to many lenders on a take-it-or-leave-it basis) when the placement has a fairly high rating and standard terms, when the issuer is relatively well known and has no unusual corporate or financial structure, when the issuer does not insist on confidentiality or unusual speed, and when the agent has the means to distribute broadly at low cost.

The style at the other end of the spectrum, negotiating terms with one or a few lenders, is most likely for placements that are highly complex or that require confidentiality, speed, or that are motivated in part by the borrower's desire to establish a relationship.

A common hybrid style involves initial negotiations with one or a few potential lead lenders, followed by an offering to many lenders once a lead has been obtained. This style is most common for placements with some complexity, so that the signal provided by the lead's commitment is important, but in which the borrower does not insist on confidentiality nor on speed.

In general, the choice of design and distribution style is the outcome of the complex decision problem previously described. Styles vary widely because the circumstances surrounding individual private placements vary widely. The examples given here hint at, but do not fully capture, the diversity of styles.

Value Added by Agents' Design and Distribution. Agents are used primarily because they have the knowledge, expertise, and organization to place securities on terms more favorable (even after subtracting their fees) than the borrower itself could obtain. Some borrowers acting alone might locate willing lenders at only moderate cost, but they could be at a disadvantage in negotiations because the lenders might assume that, should negotiations break down, the borrower would find locating additional lenders costly. Agents' activities increase the efficiency of capital markets because, in effect, they heighten competition among lenders and reduce the total costs of borrowing.

Strategic Implications of Distribution Methods for Agents. As we have argued, some agents may specialize in serving certain kinds of private placement clients (for example, middle-market companies) because their organizations' relation- ship officers, the primary source of clients, specialize in serving those clients. To some extent, agents also specialize in styles of distribution.

Such specialization both influences and is influenced by specialization in types of clients.

All private placement agents can perform the standard varieties of design and distribution, in which they send offer memos and term sheets to some number of potential lenders and then negotiate with those lenders. One avenue of specialization involves the identity of the lenders an agent ordinarily deals with. Because large insurance companies often find focusing their limited staff time on large or complex placements more profitable, agents that advise on mainly smaller issues may find maintaining close relation- ships with midsized and smaller lenders more profitable. Conversely, agents that tend to advise on large and complex placements may deal mainly with the largest life insurance companies. A sophisticated borrower surveying the field of agents may find it most advantageous to choose one that frequently deals with appropriate lenders.

A more recent variety of specialization involves the use of public bond sales forces to offer private placements on a take-it-or-leave-it basis to a large number of potential buyers. At present, only a few agents use this method and only for some of the placements on which they work. The relationship officers of these agents provide a steady stream of clients issuing the kind of highly rated, relatively standard placements that are most amenable to distribution on a take-it-or-leave-it basis. According to market participants, such agents apparently are mainly large investment banks. Few, if any, commercial banks appear to use the method at this time.

Economies of scope between agenting and public debt underwriting do not appear to be enormous. All of the top ten private debt agents listed in table 10 are either investment banks or commercial banks with agents located in securities subsidiaries with debt underwriting powers.

However, five of the agents ranked in the next tier of ten had either no securities subsidiary or one with limited powers. Thus, an organization can have a substantial agenting business without also being able to act as underwriter.

Lender Due Diligence and Contract Writing

After enough lenders have circled a deal to make it fully subscribed, the final phases of the private issuance process begin. First, lenders that circled verify the information on which they based their commitments. Large lenders conduct relatively extensive investigations that include trips to the borrower's facility (small lenders may again rely on the lead). If the investigations are satisfactory, formal letters of commitment to lend are dispatched. If lenders find material omissions or misrepresentations, either the deal falls apart or negotiations are reopened.

Following formal commitments, by convention the lead lender nominates a bond counsel to act as the lenders' representative in negotiating the detailed language of the debt contract The bond counsel is paid by the borrower, which retains its own counsel to assist in negotiations. The agent often also assists in negotiations Closing or settlement concludes the process of issuance. The documents are signed, and funds are disbursed to the borrower and the agent.

Information Flows

The private placement program is rife with information problems. As noted in part 1, the risks of lending to private market borrowers are often hard to observe and to control because relatively little public information may be available about them and because their businesses, corporate structures, or financings may be complex.

The lack of publicly available, timely information about the terms of private debt, including prices and other market conditions, is another information problem. Such information is valuable, and the collection, processing, and sale of it to borrowers is the primary business of agents.

Lenders, however, also need such information, and agents are involved in transmission of information to them as well.

CHAPTER 5

How Agents Gather Market Information

Agents can learn about current market conditions in four major ways: by observing deals in which they participate, by asking lenders, by asking other agents, and by subscribing to newsletters and other information clearinghouses.

Observation of deals in which an agent participates is most reliable, as the agent sees a offers and counteroffers and knows all details of the initial and final terms of the debt contract.

However, a large flow of deals with a variety of credit ratings and levels of complexity is required to support a constant reading of current prices and terms for the spectrum of private placement contracts. According to indications from market participants, even agents with very large volumes of business rely on multiple sources of information, not just on their own deals.

Agents also ask lenders about the terms of deals in progress and about completed deals. Such inquiries are perhaps the primary way that small agents keep up with market conditions. Lenders have mixed incentives to share information. On the one hand, judicious limits on the flow of information to agents may give lenders an advantage in negotiations. On the other hand, lenders also want information from agents and thus will enter into informal sharing arrangements with them. Lenders also cultivate agents, especially those doing a large volume of business, because they want to be offered securities and to be placed at the beginning of the queue in sequential distributions. Lenders can reward agents by responding promptly to offers, by not imposing nuisance costs while deals are in progress, and by sharing information. Because they have the most to gain by cultivating large agents, which have both the largest flow of deals to offer and the best information, lenders are most likely to share information with them. Apparently, agents seldom share information with one another, perhaps because they are in competition.

In recent years, several newsletters, and other publicly available sources of information about private market deals have appeared. None offers a complete picture of the market, and some offer information that is slightly dated. However, market participants indicated that they do gather information from these sources and find it useful. The newsletters themselves gather information by asking lenders and agents (and sometimes borrowers) about deals recently completed and those in progress.

Interestingly, some lenders reportedly seldom share information with the newsletters. This situation is consistent with their incentives to share information only with agents from which they expect favors in return. Agents also have incentives to limit information flows, but these are not so strong as the incentives of lenders. At the margin, the interest of agents may be to increase the efficiency of the private market, as improvements in terms available to borrowers (due to improved information flows) may increase the flow of deals. However, large agents may lose some of their informational advantage from such an improvement in efficiency.

How Lenders Gather Information

Lenders' sources of information are similar to those of agents, but lenders have an advantage in that they observe not only the terms of debt contracts that they buy but also at least the initial terms of all contracts they are offered. Many of the larger private market lenders we interviewed stated that they are offered many more than 500 deals in a typical year but that they purchase only a small percentage of them. They could reduce their prescreening costs by specifying more precisely to agents the kinds of deals they will buy; however, doing so would reduce the size of their window on current market conditions.

Several market participants mentioned that private market lenders actively lobby agents to offer them every deal and are unhappy with agents that fail to do so.

Lenders also gather information from agents, typically by inquiring about the final terms of deals they were offered but did not participate in. They may also make such inquiries of other lenders, though the sense of market participants' comments was that these inquiries are less frequent. Newsletters do not appear to be a primary source of information about market conditions.

Economies of Scale

Besides being able to spread fixed costs of performing agent operations over a larger volume of business, large agents (and large lenders) have an advantage in gathering the information required to operate in the private placement market. Not only are they able to glean more information directly from deals they participate in, but they have more to trade when making inquiries of other lenders and agents. Such economies of scale may translate into larger profits. They may also act as a barrier to entry of new agents, as such agents will typically have neither large deal flows nor information to trade. The effect on the profit differential between large and small lenders may be less significant, because large lenders tend to be lead lenders and small lenders can free-ride by buying pieces of the deals the large lenders commit to buy.

Since data on the costs and profitability of agents are not available, quantitative evidence of economies of scale and on the competitiveness of the agent market is limited. However, economies of scale often foster concentration of an industry, and the agenting industry is somewhat concentrated. In 1991, the top five agents of debt had 41 percent of the market by volume, the top ten had 65 percent, and the top twenty had 89 percent. Of course, as discussed earlier, such concentration could result from a combination of economies of scope and concentration in the markets for other financial services.

Price Determination

As noted, previously, the prices of private market securities are determined primarily by negotiation. In the case of securities distributed on a non- negotiable basis by fixed-income (public bond) sales forces, the negotiations are implicit in that the agent uses information about market conditions to set a price. This section briefly discusses the mechanics of price determination and the methods that agents and lenders use to set initial and reservation prices.

In most cases, term sheets for private offerings do not include a price or a rate spread over Treasury securities of comparable maturity. 142 When they send a term sheet, agents often orally suggest a price range to potential lenders. Lenders that circle the deal will circle the terms they accept on the term sheet, suggest alternatives for those they do not accept, and state a rate spread and a quantity they will purchase at that spread. The spread and terms may then become the subject of negotiations, or the agent may simply reject or accept the counteroffer. The agent collects counteroffers (the circles) and negotiates until it and the issuer decide that the deal is fully subscribed, at which point investors are notified whether they are in or out of the deal and a coupon rate is set (based on that day's Treasury yield curve and the largest spread among the counteroffers to be accepted). Lenders are thus exposed to a form of interest rate risk during the period between notification of acceptance of their circle and closing. If they hedge risks associated with a circled deal and the deal falls through, they are left with the risk associated with the hedge.

Clearly lenders will sometimes have an incentive to back out of a deal during the period between circling and commitment (if interest rates rise), but conventions in the market discourage this action. In general, lenders can pull out of a circled deal without damage to their reputations only if they discover discrepancies when performing their own due diligence.

Agents determine initial prices by various methods. An obvious method is to use spreads for recently issued private placements of comparable risk and maturity. However, partly because private placements are often tailored contracts, the private market is thin enough for some risk levels and maturities so that there may be no comparable recently issued privates. Thus, agents often look for comparable publicly issued corporate debt (especially in investment-grade deals), marking up spreads by their estimate of the public-private differential. Participants' estimates of the average differential are in the range of 10 to 40 basis points for investment-grade securities. A few agents use formal pricing models in their exercises, but comments made in interviews suggest that these are generally used as supplements rather than as primary determinants of prices.

Lenders conduct similar exercises to determine market prices but also must determine reservation prices. At some insurance companies, this determination is effectively done by portfolio managers in a part of the organization separate from that responsible for buying privates. In some cases, portfolio managers mainly compare the returns available from different classes of investments, taking diversification into account. In other cases, they compute required levels of risk-adjusted return on equity and then specify some form of demand schedule to the private placement group. A demand schedule may be as simple as a target volume of private placement purchases in each risk class for a given year, at the best available market prices, or as complicated as explicit required rate of return on equity with quantity constraints attached.

Agents' Fees and Other Costs of Issuance

Issuers generally agree in advance to pay the agent a fixed percentage of the face amount of an issue at closing. The fee is thus contingent on successful issuance.

We have little quantitative evidence about fees. Market participants agreed that fees vary with the quality and complexity of a financing. Low-rated or complex deals require more analysis and are more difficult to distribute and shepherd through the lender due diligence and final negotiation stages. Also, percentages vary inversely with deal size. Agents' costs have a large fixed component that is independent of deal size, and thus agents must earn a larger percentage of small deals.

For a $100 million straightforward A-rated private issue, market participants gave fee estimates that ranged from 3/8 to 5/8 percentage point, with the most common answer being 50 basis points. Estimates ranged widely for complex or small issues, up to several percentage points.

Many participants stated that fees have fallen slightly in recent years.

Issuers bear other fixed costs of issuance. Besides the opportunity costs of cooperating with due diligence by agents and lenders, issuers must pay the lenders' bond counsel and typically must also retain their own counsel and pay other miscellaneous costs associated with negotiations. Market participants' estimates of these costs varied widely, but for straightforward issues were often between $50,000 and $125,000, or 5 to 13 basis points for a $100 million issue.

Private Market Efficiency

In considering the efficiency of the private placement market, we focus on whether lenders or agents earn either subnormal or supranormal profits. Quantitative data on which precise judgments might be based are not available, but the comments of market participants suggest that the market is relatively efficient.

With regard to lenders' profits, one major insurance company stated recently in a public forum that interest rates on its private originations during 1989-91 were, on average, 31 basis points higher than rates on comparable public issues and that 18 basis points of this differential were spent on costs of origination and monitoring. These numbers leave 13 basis points for profit and for compensation for the reduced liquidity of private placements relative to that of publicly issued bonds. Another major company displayed proprietary data during interviews indicating that recent historical net loss rates due to defaults on private placements have been similar to loss rates on comparably rated public issues.

Presuming that these data are accurate and reasonably typical of private market lenders' experience, and assuming that lenders do not make subnormal or supranormal profits on their public bond market activities, the data place rough boundaries on the degree of private market inefficiency that may exist. The key question is the size of the differential required to compensate lenders for the relative illiquidity of private placements. If this differential is near zero, then private lenders may be making modest excess profits. 144 If the differential is near 13 basis points, then lenders are taking a modest loss at the margin. Regardless, the dollar sums involved apparently cannot be large enough to represent extraordinary inefficiencies that would be a major concern to policymakers.

Agents' profits are even harder to estimate, as no information is available about their costs.

Based on market participants' remarks about fees and staff sizes and on publicly available information about the volume of issues assisted by particular agents, the largest agents may be earning substantial marginal profits on the staff and overhead costs of their private placement groups alone. However, portions of these profits must be attributed to the actions of relationship officers and other divisions of commercial banks and investment banks, so actual profit rates may not be unusual.

Smaller agents may also be able to make profits if their flow of business is reasonably steady. As noted, smaller agents will find maintaining their knowledge of market conditions more expensive and difficult, and they will face minimum fixed costs of maintaining a staff.

We have no reason to think that agents make large excess profits, and many market participants remarked on the substantial competition that exists. On the whole, the private placement market appears to be reasonably efficient, although it may not always react quickly to changes in conditions.

Private Placements without an Agent

Data are not available on the volume of private placements issued without an agent's assistance, but it is probably substantial. Estimates by major private market lenders suggest that as much as one-third of total private issuance is done without an agent. In most cases, such issues are sold by a company that has previously borrowed in the private market and sold to investors that bought parts of the previous placements.

In such cases, some of the services that agents provide are not relevant.

For example, due diligence by the agent adds little or no value, as monitoring by the lenders since the previous issuance has kept them informed about the borrower. Locating appropriate potential lenders is also virtually costless for the borrower. Apparently, the other services provided by the agent—notably, help in negotiating terms—are thought by some issuers not to be worth the fee. Many repeat borrowers do use an agent, however, so either circumstances or opinions differ across repeat borrowers.

Agent Operations under Rule 144A

As noted in part 2, section 1, the market for many new private issues made under Rule 144A operates much more like the market for new public issues than like the traditional private placement market. Some securities involved in transactions exempt from registration under Rule 144A have been distributed by agents in the fashion described above. Others, especially those of well-known U.S. or foreign companies, have been formally underwritten.

Agent prospecting, advice, competition, and due diligence are much the same for both underwritten and traditional privates, but the distribution of underwritten securities is usually similar to that seen in the public market. Underwritten securities are often sold to typical buyers of public issues.

For example, many life insurance companies buy such issues through their public bond investment groups, not through their private placement investment groups.

When there is no firm-commitment underwriting, some Rule 144A offerings are made on a take-it-or-leave-it basis by the agent organization's fixed-income sales force. Thus, Rule 144A place- ment distributions are often at the public-like end of the spectrum of private market distribution styles. Agents that are proficient at this style of distribution have a distinct competitive advantage in assisting Rule 144A placements.

Agents are a key part of the market for privately placed debt. They gather, process, and sell information that would be prohibitively expensive for many issuers themselves to collect. They help enforce norms of behavior for borrowers and lenders that make the private market function more efficiently.

Agenting appears to be associated with economies of scale and scope that confer a distinct advantage on the large commercial banks and investment banks that specialize in serving the corporate finance needs of middle-market and large companies. Economies of scope of agenting apparently occur with other corporate finance service activities, in that bank and investment bank relationship officers can provide a stream of clients to agents while selling other products.

Economies of scale arise from fixed costs of maintaining a staff of agents and from the information sources in the private market, which are such that costs of collecting information fall as the volume of an agent's business rises.

That agenting appears to be a competitive business with low barriers to entry implies that the profits available to new or small agents are not large. Slow trends of falling information costs and increasing information flows will likely increase competition among agents even more and will improve the efficiency of the private placement market as a whole.

CHAPTER 6

Credit Crunches

Credit crunches have long been an interesting and controversial topic, partly because producing compelling evidence that a crunch occurred is often difficult. For the recent private placement credit crunch, relatively extensive evidence is available. The causes of the crunch are intertwined with the intermediated and information-intensive nature of the private market and are somewhat different from the mechanisms said to be responsible for a possible concurrent crunch in the bank loan market. The story of the private placement credit crunch sheds additional light on the economics of the private market and of financial intermediation.

The role of banks in the capital markets has changed substantially during the past twenty years: The rise of the commercial paper market and other markets is associated with a decline in the share of bank loans in all debt financings. As the bank loan and the private placement market are information- intensive and as medium-sized companies are responsible for a large share of borrowings in both markets, the two markets may be in competition, and one may come to dominate. However, we find the latter possibility unlikely. Because the focus of banks on relatively short-term lending appears to result from the maturity of their liabilities, they probably will not eclipse the private market as a source of long-term loans to information- problematic borrowers unless the structure of their liabilities changes in a major way. Repeal of the laws governing the separation of banking and other forms of commerce seems to be only a first step in such a change. For similar reasons, traditional buyers of private placements appear unlikely to become major short-term lenders.

Finally, neither commercial banks nor investment banks seem to possess a competitive advantage that would allow them to dominate the market for private placement agent services.

Credit Crunch in the Private Placement Market

Since the middle of 1990, issuers of below- investment-grade securities have encountered a sharp contraction in the availability of credit in the private placement market. A sharp rise in interest rate spreads on these securities indicates that the reduction in supply has been larger than any decline in credit demand associated with the weak economy. This credit crunch has resulted mainly from a greater reluctance of life insurance companies to assume below-investment-grade credit risk.

This reluctance is due mostly to concerns that high balance sheet proportions of such investments could lead to a runoff (or even a run) of liabilities and threaten the profitability and, perhaps, even the survival of insurance companies. Asset quality problems at many life insurances companies, regulatory changes, and runs at a few insurance companies have contributed to the reluctance of insurance companies to buy below- investment- grade private placements.

The reduced availability of credit from life insurance companies has likely adversely affected the ability of below-investment-grade companies to obtain financing. Few alternative lenders have entered or expanded their presence in the below- investment-grade sector of the private market to fill the void. The reason appears to center on the high start-up costs that potential lenders must incur to enter the private market. Also, the number of alternatives to private placements is limited.

Although they may be the main practical alternative, bank loans are far from perfect substitutes, and some firms shut out of the private market may have found banks to be reluctant lenders.

Definition of Credit Crunch

Many definitions of the term credit crunch have appeared in the literature. In our view, a credit crunch occurs when, for a given price of credit, lenders substantially reduce the volume of credit provided to a group of borrowers whose risk is essentially unchanged. That is, a credit crunch is caused by a reduction in lenders' willingness to make risky investments or by a "flight to quality" by lenders. In terms of a standard supply and demand diagram, a credit crunch is a substantial decline in the volume of credit caused mainly by a leftward shift of the credit supply curve, when the shift is not due principally to an increase in the riskiness of borrowers. This definition is similar in spirit to that of Bernanke and Lown (1991), who define a crunch as "a significant leftward shift in the supply for bank loans, holding constant both the safe real interest rate and the quality of potential borrowers."

A contraction of supply alone does not necessarily imply a credit crunch, as credit availability may decrease and lending terms tighten because of an increase in the riskiness of borrowers. Thus, our definition of a credit crunch does not include a reduction in supply that is a normal response to a recession or an economic slowdown. In such circumstances, the riskiness of borrowers normally increases, and lenders demand compensation either in higher interest rates or in tighter nonprice terms of loans. Although borrowers might characterize such a reduction in credit supply as a credit crunch, such a characterization would not be appropriate because the decrease in credit is a normal response of lenders to changing economic conditions. Cantor and Wenninger (1993) refer to this situation as a "credit slowdown."

Our definition of credit crunch differs from some, notably that of Owens and Schreft (1992), in that it does not require that the reduction in credit be accomplished by nonprice rationing. The reduction may be affected entirely by an increase in the relative price of credit, as would normally occur in response to a leftward shift of a supply curve, or by some combination of price increase and nonprice rationing.

Evidence Showing Credit Crunch Occurred

Recent events in the below-investment-grade segment of the private placement market qualify as a credit crunch because gross issuance or originations for below- investment-grade debt declined substantially and spreads on such debt increased sharply, whereas spreads on investment- grade private placements held steady or declined. A general increase in the riskiness of borrowers cannot account for these phenomena. The decline of issuance may have been accomplished partly by nonprice rationing, but we have no quantitative evidence to support such a claim, and market participants' remarks about nonprice rationing were mixed.

Data from three separate sources confirm a reduction in issuance of below-investment-grade private placements. First, gross issuance by below-investment- grade, nonfinancial corporations fell more than 50 percent in 1991, a much steeper drop than that seen in issuance by investment- grade corporations. 147 As a percentage of gross offerings, below-investment-grade issuance declined from 16 percent in

1990 to 9 percent in 1991. Data for 1992 indicate that issuance remained depressed, although the percentage was slightly above that in 1991. Second, although total commitments by major life insurance companies to purchase private placements remained roughly constant from early 1990 through mid-1992, the proportion of below investment- grade issues dropped sharply in the middle of 1990, from 21 percent in the first half of 1990 to 11 percent in the second half of that year. Since then, the percentage has varied between 31/2 percent and 71/2 percent. 148 Third, the reduced rate of gross purchases indicated by the survey is also evident in insurance companies' holdings of below-investment-grade securities. Holdings of such securities at all life insurers fell 11 percent in 1991, whereas holdings of investment-grade securities rose nearly 12 percent. As a result, speculative-grade private bonds as a percentage of all private placements in insurance company portfolios declined from 19.8 percent in 1990 to 16.7 percent in 1991. The low rate of commitments to purchase below-grade private placements in 1992 led to a further decline in their share to 15.3 percent last year.

Accompanying the decline in gross issuance and outstanding has been a sharp increase in yield spreads on below-investment-grade private placements. According to market reports, before 1990 the difference between yields on BB- and BBB-rated private placements with comparable terms was about 100 basis points; since then, the difference has been as high as 250 basis points. 149 Although data are unavailable for periods before 1990, the relative movement in yields on BB and BBB private bonds is confirmed in the spreads reported in the ACLI survey (charts 17 and 18). 150 During the first half of 1990, the spread between yields on BB private placements and comparable Treasury securities was about 300 basis points, compared with 190 basis points on BBB private placements. From that time, the spread on BB bonds moved up to almost 425 basis points in the second quarter of 1991, but more recently it has retreated to around 350 basis points. During the same period the BBB spread drifted down to 180 basis points. Similarly, the spread on A-rated private placements varied little over the past three years.

The substantial increase in spreads over Treasuries for BB private placements cannot plausibly be attributed to a general increase in risk associated with the slowdown in economic activity because such an increase in risk should have also led to an increase in BBB spreads. In fact, those spreads declined. Similarly, although the slow- down might have caused issues to be more concentrated at the low-quality end of the risk range that each rating category spans, leading to an increase in average spreads for each rating category, such a mechanism should have affected both BB and BBB spreads. The data thus indicate that, within the below- investment-grade segment of the private placement market, for a given level of risk loan prices went up whereas the volume of loans went down. These facts support our assertion that a credit crunch occurred within that market segment.

Sources of the Credit Crunch

A credit crunch can occur for several reasons. It may result from actions taken by regulators that affect lenders' ability or incentive to assume certain risks. It may result also from internal developments at lending institutions, such as unexpectedly large loan losses, that cause portfolio rebalancing involving greater conservatism in lending. For lenders that are financial intermediaries, a credit crunch may result from liability holders' becoming concerned about the intermediaries' financial condition. The ability of intermediaries to raise funds to support their investment activity may be adversely affected in such circumstances and may lead to their adoption of more conservative investment strategies to restore public confidence. The latter mechanism appears to have been primarily responsible for the crunch in the private placement market Problems of asset quality at life insurance companies, a change in regulatory reporting requirements, and runs on a few insurers combined to raise doubts about the solvency and liquidity of insurance companies and to focus the public's and the rating agencies' attention on the proportion of an insurer's assets invested in below-investment-grade securities as a signal of its solvency.

Publicity about high proportions of poorly performing commercial mortgages in insurance company portfolios was one event raising doubts among the public about the solvency of insurers. Commercial mortgages make up 25 percent of general account assets at the twenty largest insurance companies, which include most of the major participants in the private placement market. Additional exposure to commercial real estate risks comes from direct real estate investments, which at many life insurance companies consist primarily of real-estate- related limited partnerships. As the press has widely reported, delinquency and foreclosure rates on these commercial real estate investments have risen sharply over the past few years. These problems heightened public awareness of the financial problems of life insurance companies and thus added to the pressure on those with significant holdings of commercial real estate loans to shift out of all lower-quality assets. Also, since even sound commercial real estate loans turned out to be riskier than anticipated when they were made, life insurance companies shifted investments toward high- quality assets.

Publicity about losses on some publicly issued junk bonds also raised concerns about the quality of below-investment-grade securities in general, and a change in regulatory reporting requirements made insurance companies' holdings of such assets seem to have increased. In June 1990, the National Association of Insurance Commissioners (NAIC) introduced finer distinctions in its credit ratings of corporate bonds, including private placements. Under the old rating system, many securities, especially public bonds, with credit quality equivalent to BB or B received an investment-grade rating. To correct this shortcoming, the NAIC adopted a system with categories more closely aligned with those in the public market (table 13). NAIC- 1, the top rating, was given to securities rated AAA to A; NAIC-2 to BBB securities; NAIC-3 to BB securities; and NAIC-4 to B securities. Although insurers' actual holdings were probably little changed, the reclassification resulting from the new system caused insurers' reported holdings of below-investment- grade bonds, both private and public, to rise between 1989 and 1990 from 15 percent of total bond holdings to 21 percent. The level of reported holdings of high-yield bonds jumped more than 40 percent.

The sudden appearance of a much-increased percentage of below-investment-grade securities on the balance sheets of life insurance companies focused the attention of policyholders and other holders of insurance company liabilities on the composition of insurers' bond holdings. As evidence of increased public sensitivity, a recent study by Fenn and Cole (forthcoming) found that stock prices of insurance companies with high concentrations of junk bonds were adversely affected in early 1990 by the publicity surrounding the financial problems of First Executive, whose insurance units subsequently failed because of losses on junk bonds. In contrast, stock prices of insurance companies with little exposure to junk bonds were not affected. The public's greater sensitivity to the quality of life insurance companies' assets discouraged many insurers from purchasing lower-quality private placements from fear of losing insurance business to competitors with lower proportions of below-investment-grade bonds in their portfolios.

That public fears regarding below-investment- grade private placements were warranted is not clear, as market participants report that loss rates on those securities have not been unusual. Loss rates on such securities may be expected to differ from those on similarly rated public junk bonds because private placements typically contain covenants or collateral and because only a few information-intensive lenders are involved; thus, corrective actions are timelier, and workouts are less difficult. Because nonparticipants lack a clear understanding of the private market, however, the public has a tendency to equate below-investment- grade private placements with public junk bonds.

Another development pressuring insurance companies to restrict purchases of below- investment-grade private placements have been the concern of credit rating agencies about the lack of liquidity of private placements, especially those that are below investment grade. This concern appears to be a consequence of the July 1991 collapse of Mutual Benefit, which lacked the liquidity needed to meet heavy redemptions by policyholders. Driven by a fear of being down- graded, insurance companies have sought more liquidity in their bond portfolios by concentrating on higher-grade credits, which are more readily sold in the secondary market.

Another regulatory move by the NAIC appears not to have been a significant cause of the crunch. This move involved changes in the mandatory securities valuation reserves (MSVR) held against bonds in life insurance company portfolios. For bonds that would have been rated investment grade under the old rating system, but fell to NAIC-3 or NAIC-4 under the new system, required reserves jumped from 2 percent of the bonds' statement values to 5 percent for NAIC-3 and 10 percent for NAIC- 4. 153 Also, the time allowed to reach the mandatory reserve levels was shortened. At year-end 1991, however, all of the twenty largest life insurance companies had MSVRs that were more than adequate to meet the fully phased-in standards.

The individual importance of these factors as causes of the credit crunch is hard to isolate. They are, however, interrelated. For example, the effect of the new NAIC rating system probably would have been much smaller had insurance companies not experienced problems with commercial real estate loans. Futhermore, the new rating system, combined with the failure of First Executive, focused public attention on below- investment- grade private placements as an asset that could add to the industry's financial problems. In any case, the main impetus behind the credit crunch has been life insurance companies' fears that liability holders might lose confidence in them and redeem insurance policies, annuities, and guaranteed investment contracts should they exhibit above-average holdings of below-investment-grade securities.

Prospects for an Easing of the Crunch

As a group, life insurance companies are unlikely to resume investing in below-investment-grade private placements at pre-1990 levels until their asset problems have improved and public concern about the health of the industry has appreciably diminished. As this improvement hinges mainly on a recovery of the commercial real estate market, many analysts expect that insurers will, for the foreseeable future, remain reluctant to provide funds to the low-grade sector of the private market. This prospect has already led some insurers to cut staff and to reduce resources devoted to credit evaluation and monitoring. If the cutbacks become widespread, the long-run ability of the insurance industry to supply credit to medium-sized, below-investment-grade companies could be impaired.

Risk-based capital standards, which become effective at the end of 1993, could reinforce the reluctance of insurance companies to buy below- investment-grade securities. The new standards are aimed at measuring the prudential adequacy of insurers' capital as a means of distinguishing between weakly capitalized and strongly capitalized companies. To this end, insurance companies will report the ratios of their book capital to levels of capital that are adjusted for risk. As an insurer's ratio falls progressively below one, successively stronger regulatory actions will be triggered.

In the current environment, most insurers will probably attempt to achieve ratios in excess of one. One way they can raise their risk-based capital ratios is to shift into low-risk assets. In this regard, below-investment-grade securities carry risk weights much higher than those on investment-grade bonds and even those on commercial mortgages. Over time, however, as the financial condition of insurance companies improves and public concern about their health recedes, insurers will be more inclined to consider risk-adjusted returns in reaching investment decisions and thus may allocate a greater proportion of assets to higher-risk categories, such as below-investment-grade bonds.

Despite the almost three-year absence of insurance companies from the below-investment- grade sector and the persistence of unusually high spreads, new lenders have not picked up much of the slack in the private placement market, primarily because of the high start¬up costs of entering the market. Long-term investments in expensive internal monitoring systems and staffs of credit analysts, lawyers, and workout specialists are required. Also, the market operates largely on the basis of unwritten, informal rules enforced by the desire of major agents and buyers to maintain their reputations. Thus, to an outsider, the way the market operates may be hard to understand. Being a newcomer to the market with no established reputation may involve costs. These factors may inhibit outside investors from risking their money in this market.

State and large corporate pension funds are natural candidates to fill the gap left by the insurance companies in the private market because of their demand for fixed- rate investments. Many pension funds, however, have charters that prevent them from investing in below- investment-grade or illiquid assets. Most pension fund managers are also reportedly reluctant to invest in an unfamiliar market. Because pension funds generally lack the necessary capabilities for due diligence and monitoring, their managers have difficulty familiarizing themselves with the private market by making small initial investments. A decision to invest in below-investment-grade private placements involves a significant long-term commitment of resources that few pension fund managers appear to find attractive. In the case of state pension funds, even if they wished to invest, many would face problems in hiring the necessary personnel because state legislatures generally control staff sizes and salaries. Any attempt by state pension funds to hire large numbers of credit analysts thus could run into political obstacles.

Pension funds (and others) might quickly enter the private market by investing in funds managed by professional private placement investors.

Several funds have been formed in the past two years, but they are unlikely to operate on a scale sufficient to fill the void left by the insurance companies. Pension fund managers appear reluctant to invest even indirectly in a market with which they are unfamiliar. In addition, some are concerned that fund managers would not monitor borrowers with sufficient diligence. Also, insurance companies, which would be the primary source of the managerial resources necessary for operating of managed private placement funds, have thus far not set up funds on a large scale, even though some companies currently have excess capacity to analyze and monitor lower- quality credits. Some are unwilling to make a long-term commitment of resources to this effort because they expect eventually to resume investing in below-investment-grade private placement for their own accounts. Finally, most institutional investors would expect insurance companies acting as investment managers to purchase some of the securities for their own accounts. Such a requirement lessens the incentive to establish managed funds because of insurers' current aversion to purchasing below-investment-grade bonds.

Finance companies face much smaller start-up costs than pension funds do, but their participation has traditionally been in the highest-risk segment of the private placement market, a segment in which life insurance companies have not generally been active. Insurers typically have made unsecured loans, mainly to the highest-quality speculative-grade borrowers. In contrast, finance companies specialize in secured lending, normally with equity features attached. Thus, the risk-return profile of the typical insurance company borrower does not suit finance companies, nor would such borrowers generally find finance companies' terms attractive. In addition, several finance companies that were significant lenders in the private market have reduced their lending to low-rated firms because they have been faced with credit problems of their own.

Marginal increases in the number of lenders and in their commitments to below-investment-grade private placements may not have much effect on the credit crunch. With only a few lenders remaining in this segment of the market, and with most of these willing to lend only a limited amount to any one borrower, agents often have difficulty putting together a syndicate of lenders sufficient to purchase even medium-sized issues. Because the agents must incur fixed costs before a deal can be proved viable, and because they are paid only upon success, most agents have also withdrawn from the below-investment-grade segment of the market. This situation explains an apparent paradox: Those few remaining, willing lenders sometimes complain that not enough prospective issues are coming to market to permit them to lend all their funds available for below-investment-grade borrowers. Thus, the crunch may disappear only with a wholesale return of life insurance companies to this market segment or with the entry of a significant number of new lenders.

One development that may have eased the crunch for a few borrowers is the increased frequency of ratings of private placements by major rating agencies. Issuers on the cusp between a NAIC-2 and NAIC-3 often obtain ratings from one of the agencies before seeking ratings from the NAIC. Because the agencies charge higher fees for ratings than does the NAIC and are less overworked, they can often gather more information and conduct more extensive analyses, which sometimes justify investment-grade ratings. 154 The

NAIC generally accepts such ratings but reserves the right to overrule them.

Credit Crunch Effect and Alternatives For Borrowers

The effect of this credit crunch on the economic activity of potential borrowers is impossible to assess with any precision. As private placements are seldom the vehicle for providing day-to-day working capital, it seems unlikely that many potential borrowers have failed because of a lack of financing. Private placements often provide funds for expansion, however, and the growth of some medium-sized businesses possibly has been constrained by this credit crunch. According to market participants, one rationale for private issuance is not only to lengthen the maturity of their debt but also to loosen constraints imposed by the collateral requirements typical of bank loans. Many medium-sized borrowers can obtain bank loans only in amounts up to 50 percent of finished inventory and 80 percent of eligible receivables. Often, upon reaching those limits, borrowers have issued an unsecured private placement, used part of the proceeds to pay down the bank debt, and used the remaining proceeds and new bank debt to finance expansion.

With that course no longer open, low-rated borrowers must attempt to find other sources of capital. The bank loan market seems to be the first alternative for many lower-rated borrowers.

Although market participants disagree somewhat, most report that the credit problems at commercial banks have caused these banks to limit lending, to tighten terms as lines have come up for renewal, or even to eliminate lines of credit. This view is confirmed by the surveys of the lending terms of large banks periodically undertaken by the Federal Reserve System. Furthermore, some insurance companies have reportedly had to increase their loans to existing borrowers whose credit lines have been cut by their commercial banks.

Some low-rated companies have taken advantage of favorable stock market conditions in 1991 and 1992 and issued equity. In some cases, the reduced leverage resulting from equity injections has raised issuers' credit ratings to investment grade, and has given them renewed access to the private bond market. Alternatively, some firms have attached credit enhancements to their private placements to move up to an investment-grade rating. The public junk bond market, despite its revival in the latter half of 1991, has been a source of funds for only a few companies, as the typical below-investment-grade private issue is generally too small and too complex a credit for the public market.

The market for privately placed debt is served by lenders that are financial intermediaries. As such, the market is vulnerable to breakdowns, which occur when those who provide funds to the financial intermediaries are no longer willing to do so or when intermediaries become sensitive to the threat of such a withdrawal. This mechanism appears to be the main one behind the recent credit crunch for below-investment-grade borrowers.

The conditions causing the breakdown in financial intermediation at life insurance companies appear unlikely to ease significantly in the near future. With other lenders and markets unable to fully accommodate the financing needs of the medium-sized, below- investment-grade companies that are most affected, those companies may for several more years have more difficulty than usual in financing expansions.

CHAPTER 7

The Current and Prospective Roles of Commercial Banks

Commercial banks participate in the private placement market as issuers, buyers, and agents. They also compete with private market lenders in providing credit Drawing on parts 1 and 2, this section describes the current role of banks in the private placement market and speculates about their role in the future.

Banks as Agents and Brokers

U.S. commercial banks have recently been strong competitors in the market for private placement agenting services. Of the 5,550-private placements of debt appearing in the IDD database for 1989-91, U.S. commercial banks were either sole agent or co-agent for 1,944, or 35 percent. Their share of volume was 32 percent. Foreign banks had a 1 percent share of all volume. In the market for private equity agenting, U.S. banks had a 14 percent share of volume during 1990-91, whereas foreign banks had a 6 percent share.

During 1975-77, U.S. banks had only about a 7 percent share of the total private placement agenting market (Board of Governors, 1977). Their share has clearly grown substantially during the ensuing fifteen years.

Its Listed the twenty-five U.S. banks that appear as agents in the IDD database for the period 1989-91, along with the number and volume of assisted placements of both debt and equity. Two things about the list are striking. First, only ten banks accounted for 98 percent of the known volume of new issues assisted by banks.

Second, the list is relatively short when compared with the list of more than 10,000 commercial banks in the United States. The table is surely incomplete, as some banks that act as agents may not report their transactions to IDD; however, it does show that apparently only a small fraction of banks act as agents.

As a group, commercial banks do not appear to specialize in assisting types of transactions or issuers in industries that are different from those assisted by investment banks.

Regulatory restrictions may to some extent reduce banks' ability to compete in the agenting market. In particular, the few banks possessing section 20 subsidiaries with full debt and equity underwriting powers may have a competitive advantage over banks having no such powers.

Why Do Banks Act as Agents

Banks appear to enter the private placement agenting business for two reasons. First, such business can generate profitable fee income.

As noted previously, almost no data are available on agents' fee income, costs, or profits. On the basis of scanty knowledge about staff sizes and fee rates gleaned from interviews, we speculate that agenting is quite profitable for those banks doing a high volume of business. For those that assist in only a few transactions, and thus cannot capture economies of scale, agenting may be only marginally profitable.

Second, banks may act as agents as part of a strategy of offering a broad array of corporate financial services, not just loans. we argued that economies of scope exist between private placement agenting and other lines of capital market business, such as making loans or underwriting securities. The relationship officers of commercial and investment banks are the primary sources of prospective clients for private placement agenting. An institution must provide financial services to many corporate clients to generate a flow of agenting business sufficient to justify maintaining an agenting group. we provide evidence in support of this assertion. It ranks the top twenty-five U.S. bank holding companies by volume of commercial and industrial loans on the books at the end of 1991, and gives the known private placement agenting volume (debt only) for such banks during 1989-91. It is revealed, all the top ten bank agents were among the top twenty- five holders of commercial and industrial loans, and the majority of the top lenders also acted as private placement agents.

Prospective Changes in Market Share of U.S. and Foreign Banks

As noted, the agenting market share of U.S. banks has increased substantially during the past fifteen years. During interviews, market participants offered two explanations. First, as banks have lost commercial and industrial loan business to other lenders or markets, they have become increasingly interested in selling a broad array of financial services to corporations. Many have also reorganized their operations, converting loan officers into relationship officers that operate more on the investment bank model of customer relationship management. This reorganization has increased banks' efficiency at identifying potential clients for private placement agenting and at winning their business.

Second, according to some participants, investment banks had placed a lower priority on their private placement businesses during the mid-1980s and instead emphasized lines of business related to mergers and acquisitions. If true, this change may have provided banks with a window of competitive opportunity that they exploited.

Foreign banks began entering the agenting market only during the past few years. Their entrance was coincident with two events: an increase in issues of private placements by foreign borrowers and a substantial increase of foreign banks' share of the market for commercial and industrial loans. Foreign bank agents may have an advantage in winning the business of foreign borrowers. Relationship officers of foreign banks can probably market private placement agenting services in much the same way, and with much the same effectiveness, as relationship officers of U.S. banks.

Prospective changes in market share are difficult to assess. Having learned to exploit their agenting opportunities more efficiently, banks are unlikely to lose expertise or to abandon the private market.

U.S. banks may gradually lose market share if their share of all corporate financial services declines. They may gain market share if their efficiency continues to increase. Foreign banks seem likely to continue to have some presence in the agenting market, but beyond that their prospects are impossible to assess. Banks will probably not come to dominate agenting because investment banks are intent on remaining competitive.

The Role of Regulation

Banks and their subsidiaries may engage in agenting without prior permission; they are subject only to prudential supervision that focuses on ensuring disclosure of possible conflicts of interest. Bank holding companies and their nonbank subsidiaries, including section 20 (securities) subsidiaries, must obtain permission from the Federal Reserve Board to act as agents, and such agents are subject to various restrictions. See appendix C for a detailed description of legal and regulatory restrictions on the private placement agent activities of banks.

Regulatory restrictions that focus on agenting itself do not appear so far to have imposed many competitive disadvantages on banks. Limits on banks' general securities powers, however, may have imposed two disadvantages. First, banks (but not section 20 subsidiaries) are effectively prevented from acting as brokers or dealers in the secondary market for private placements because they cannot buy and sell restricted securities for their own account. As the secondary market for private placements has been relatively small to date and banks may act as riskless principals, this disadvantage has probably been minor.

Perhaps more important are Glass-Steagal restrictions on bank underwriting of new issues of public securities. Because of economies of scope between public underwriting and the distribution stage of private placement agenting, in some cases, public security sales forces can distribute private placements more efficiently than can a private placement agenting group. Only bank holding companies possessing section 20 subsidiaries with full debt powers (and full equity powers, for private equity issues) will possess such sales forces and be able to capture the cost efficiencies. Competitive pressures will cause investment banks or commercial banks with section 20 subsidiaries to win the mandate to assist most such issues.

As market participants indicated, underwriting powers may convey another, more subtle advantage. Part of the service that a financial institution typically provides is advice that leads a borrower to issue in the private market. Such advice often includes an analysis of the relative benefits of raising funds in various of markets, including the bank loan and public security markets. The advice of an institution capable of assisting financing in all the relevant markets is likely to be afforded more credibility than the advice of one that can assist only in the market it is recommending.

Credibility of advice is an important factor in the minds of many issuers as they choose an agent. Thus, banks with full securities powers actually have an advantage in this regard over investment banks that do not make nor syndicate loans, as such banks can assist in three markets (loan, private, and public), while such investment banks can assist in only two (private and public).

Conversely, banks without securities powers may in some situations be at a disadvantage.

we lists U.S. bank holding companies that had received Federal Reserve Board permission to have section 20 subsidiaries as of May 1992, the powers of those subsidiaries, and the location within the banking organization of the private placement agenting group, if any. All the banks with full securities powers have chosen to locate their agents (if any) in the section 20 subsidiary whereas, to our knowledge, only one of those with partial securities powers has chosen to do so. This difference may occur for two reasons. First, the advantages that full securities powers confer on agents may outweigh costs of the additional regulatory restrictions that are imposed when they are located in a section 20 subsidiary. Second, and perhaps more important, regulations limiting the fraction of revenue a section 20 subsidiary may earn from ineligible underwriting activity encourage the holding company to move eligible activities (which include agenting of private placements) into the section 20 subsidiary to prevent the limitations from binding.

The three largest bank agents are located in section 20 subsidiaries with full powers. However, other banks without full powers do a substantial agenting business. Thus, lack of securities powers does not seem to be an absolute barrier to agenting of private placements.

Banks as Issuers of Equity

The private placement market appears not to be an important source of equity capital for U.S. banks. Table 17 lists the private equity issues of U.S. banks during 1990-91 that appear in the IDD Information Services data base. 160 U.S. banks issued about $2 billion of equity in the private placement market during 1990-91, but $1.25 billion was in a single placement of convertible preferred stock by Citibank with a foreign investor. Only twelve individual issues appear on the list, and several of the issuers are relatively well known and presumably could issue in the public markets without great difficulty. During this period the number and total volume of issues by foreign banks was also not large.

The legal separation of banking and commerce in the United States may be one reason banks do not issue much private equity. The Bank Holding Company Act of 1956, the amendments of 1970 to that act, and Federal Reserve Board rulings prevent nonbank corporations from owning or controlling banks or bank holding companies Acquisition of more than 5 percent of the voting stock of a bank or bank holding company requires Federal Reserve Board approval. As appendix B notes, most private equity is purchased by institutional investors, especially pension funds, which tend to take large blocks of individual offerings. When a purchase would amount to more than 5 percent of a bank's total capital, costs of obtaining regulatory approval would reduce the issue's attractiveness for purchasers.

In general, the private equity market appears to serve, directly or indirectly, mainly those start-ups or other high-risk issuers that promise high returns. Such returns compensate investors for the illiquidity and monitoring costs associated with private equity. As a mature and highly regulated industry, banking may be unattractive to such investors.

Banks as Issuers of Debt

U.S. banks and bank holding companies are more active issuers in the private debt market. The IDD database lists 174 private debt issues by them during 1990-91, 97 unsecured and 77 secured, for a total of

$8.43 billion (table 19). These issues were about 5 percent of all private debt issues in the database for the period.

About a third of banks' issuance was asset- backed debt, such as mortgage-backed or receivable-backed notes. According to remarks by market participants, many such issues would have been difficult to issue publicly. Either they were a new form of instrument (for example, some receivable-backed bonds) or they required a buyer to engage in extensive due diligence and monitoring (many second-mortgage-backed bonds).

As noted in part 1, the private placement market is a proving ground for new types of instrument. If no problems surface with a new instrument (and if extensive monitoring is not required), public market investors may eventually be willing to buy it. Thus, the private placement market is important to banks and other financial institutions as an arena for testing some of their financial innovations.

we summarizes private debt issuance by foreign banks. The totals for unsecured debt are similar to those for U.S. banks, but foreign banks issued very little secured or asset-backed debt.

Banks as Buyers of Private Placements

We describes regulatory restrictions on bank purchases of private placements. To summarize, and ignoring minor exceptions, banks may not buy privately placed equity, but they may buy private debt so long as it is booked as a loan for regulatory purposes. Bank holding companies may buy limited amounts of equity and may buy privately placed debt without restriction.

Almost no data on the share of new private issues that is purchased by banks are publicly available. As part of a staff report on Rule 144A dated September 30, 1991, the SEC collected information on initial purchasers of sixty- nine Rule 144A placements issued from April 1990 through July 1991. Banks and savings and loan institutions (which were grouped together in the report) were initial purchasers of only $232 million of the $6.75 billion, or 3.44 percent of placements in the sample. They purchased only 4.16 percent of sample placements of straight debt, 7.42 percent of placements of asset- backed securities, and 0.7 percent of placements of common and preferred equity. Similarly, U.S. commercial banks purchased only about 3 percent of a different sample private placements.

The extent to which these samples are representative of all private placements is not known. As noted in appendix C, we have some reason to believe that banks may be less willing to purchase Rule 144A placements because performing normal loan-underwriting due diligence for those may be more difficult than for traditional placements.

Anecdotal evidence obtained in interviews, however, confirms that banks are infrequent buyers of private placements. According to market participants, most banks prefer investments of shorter duration than the average private placement. Relationships of issuers with buyers of placements also tend to be less close than relationships of loan borrowers with bank lenders, and banks like the opportunity to sell other services that close relationships provide. Market participants suggested that a bank is most likely to buy part of a placement when it already has a relationship with the issuer (since costs of due diligence are small).

All-in returns on private placements of debt may also be smaller for banks than for insurance companies. Most banks would probably swap the fixed-rate payment stream of a placement to match the repricing pattern of floating rate liabilities, and the cost of such swaps may make most placements unattractive to banks.

In summary, no major regulatory barriers to bank purchases of private placements of debt appear to exist, but various economic considerations may make placements less attractive than other investments to banks. Banks seem unlikely to become major buyers of private placements in the near to medium term.

Banks as Competitors of Private Placement Lenders

Although banks do not buy many private placements of debt, they do compete with buyers of private debt. Firms that can borrow in the private placement market can also typically borrow in the bank loan market. The two sources of funding are not perfect substitutes in that terms typically differ, but a sufficient cost differential can persuade borrowers to choose the alternative with otherwise less-attractive terms.

Available data do not support an empirical analysis of the extent of substitution between the two markets. Market participants indicated that the competition is greatest for borrowings at intermediate maturities of three to seven years. Private market lenders do not usually offer competitive terms at shorter maturities, and banks are not usually competitive at longer maturities. This difference in competitive advantage is most likely due to economies of scope between lending and the differing liabilities for the two classes of lenders, as part 1 discussed. Typical private market lenders have long-term, often fixed-rate liabilities and thus can make long-term loans more cheaply than can banks, which must bear the cost of swaps and other hedges. Banks are naturally most competitive for short-term, floating-rate loans.

According to market participants, at intermediate maturities, the decision between a bank loan and a placement depends on a borrower's preference for a fixed or floating rate, on the current cost of interest rate swaps, and on prevailing rates in the two markets. Rates and swap costs vary enough that a borrower's decision may be different at different times. In other words, the maturity beyond which a qualified borrower desiring a fixed rate is almost certain to go to the private placement market varies with market conditions.

No substantial change in the nature of this competition or in the comparative advantages of banks and private market lenders appears in the offing. The average maturity of insurance company liabilities has grown shorter during the last decade, making the private placement market more competitive at shorter intermediate maturities.

Differences in the maturity structures of banks and private market lenders are likely to persist, however, at least until the legal restrictions that separate banking and other forms of commerce are removed.

CHAPTER 8

Definition of Private Placement, Resales of Private Placements, and Additional Information about Rule 144A

A private placement is a security that is issued in the United States but is exempt from registration with the Securities and Exchange Commission as a result of being issued in transactions not involving any public offering. This definition is based upon legal criteria and not upon the economic characteristics of the financial instrument. For example, in an economic sense, commercial loans to businesses and private placements of debt are similar, but in a legal sense a loan is not a security and thus is not a private placement. Similarly, bank deposits are not private placements even though some are called notes and are distributed by dealers.

The legal status of a financial instrument can be economically important, however, because securities fall under the jurisdiction of securities law whereas other instruments are covered by commercial law. A significant practical difference between the two codes is that the Securities Act of 1933 (sections 12(2) and 17) provides for civil liabilities and criminal sanctions for fraud in the sale of a security. As a consequence, buyers of securities have greater protection and recourse in the event of fraud than those who make loans.

Exemptions from Registration for Private Placment Issuance

The Securities Act of 1933 requires that all offers and sales of securities be made through a registration statement filed with the Securities and Exchange Commission (SEC) unless an exemption from registration is available. Section 3 of the act exempts from registration certain types of securities, such as U.S. Treasury securities and commercial paper, and section 4 exempts certain securities transactions, such as the issuance of private placements and resales of registered securities.

More specifically, section 4(2) of the act exempts "transactions by an issuer not involving any public offering." 164 This exemption is based on the premise that sophisticated buyers of securities do not need the protection afforded by registration as they should be capable of obtaining information about the issuer on their own.

Initially issuers-based exemptions under section 4(2) on interpretations by the SEC and case law. 165 Between 1974 and 1980, the SEC adopted three rules to clarify the conditions for exemptions for offerings. In 1982, the SEC issued Regulation D, which provides a different formal basis for a private placement exemption by combining and expanding these rules.

Regulation D is a non- exclusive safe harbor, however, and most issuers have continued to rely on section 4(2), although their offerings satisfy most conditions of

Rule 506 of Regulation D.

Rule 506 offers and sales may be for any amount and to any number of accredited investors, but the issuer or its agent may not engage in any general solicitation or advertising, the investors must purchase securities for their own accounts and not for distribution to the public, and no more than thirty-five unaccredited investors may purchase the securities. Accredited investors are mainly institutional investors, but the category also includes individuals with sufficient net worth or income. The issuer must reasonably believe that unaccredited investors are capable of evaluating the investment. The rule does not require public disclosure of information about the issuer if only accredited investors are involved. However, the issuer must disclose to investors that the securities have not been registered with the SEC and that they cannot be resold unless they have been registered or the resale transaction is exempt.

Finally, the issuer must file a notice with the SEC within fifteen days of the first sale. Issuers relying on section 4(2) for an exemption generally attempt to conform to these conditions, except that they do not file a notice with the SEC.

Some private placements are issued under exemptions other than those offered by Regulation D and section 4(2). For example, section 4(6) of the 1933 act exempts issues totaling less than $5 million at one time (instead of over a twelve- month period) under some circumstances, and section 3(a)(11) exempts securities that are issued by a resident of a state who is in business in that state and that are sold only to residents of the state. The relative volumes of placements issued under the several possible exemptions are not known, but remarks by market participants indicate that most of total volume relies for exemption on section 4(2).

Exemptions from Registration for Resales of Private Placements

Sections 4(2) and Regulation D provide exemptions from registration only for issuers of private placements. Those wishing to resell registered securities can rely on section 4(1) of the Securities Act, which exempts transactions by parties other than issuers, underwriters, and dealers. This exemption is not directly available to investors in private placements, however, because such investors are technically regarded as underwriters; if they were not, private placements could be indirectly distributed to the public through resales by investors, thereby circumventing the registration requirements of the Securities Act (Davis, Polk, and Wardwell, 1990).

Exemptions for resales of private placements are provided by the informal guidelines of the so-called section 4(11/2) exemption and by SEC Rules 144 and 144A. The section 4(11/2) exemption combines sections 4(1) and 4(2) of the Securities Act, neither of which by itself is sufficient to support an exemption. This exemption, based upon SEC no-action letters and market practice, assumes that resales of private placements are permissible without registration so long as they generally satisfy the conditions necessary for an issuer to justify an exemption under section 4(2).

That is, if buyers are of the same class of investors eligible to purchase private placements from an issuer and if they indicate their intention to hold the securities for investment purposes, then the seller in the transaction can be viewed as not being an underwriter and thus can rely on section 4(1) for an exemption (Carlson, Raymond, and Keen, 1992).

Resales based on section 4(1/2) are somewhat cumbersome in that they involve letters of intent (to hold for investment purposes) from buyers to sellers.

Rule 144 permits investors to resell private placements after two years from the date of the securities' issuance, subject to certain limitations, and to sell without limitation after three years.

Rule 144A

Rule 144A, adopted by the SEC in April 1990, provides an exemption from registration for secondary market transactions in private placements in which the buyer is a sophisticated financial institution, defined in the rule as a qualified institutional buyer (QIB). The rule applies only minimal restrictions to qualifying transactions. QIBs are a subset of accredited investors; but, in any case, most private placements are purchased by QIBs, and thus the rule makes underwriting of new issues and active secondary trading feasible.

As defined by Rule 144A, QIBs are financial institutions, corporations, and partnerships that own and invest on a discretionary basis at least $100 million of securities. The scope of this definition is broad enough to include the major investors in private placements, such as life insurance companies, pension funds, investment companies, foreign and domestic banks, savings and loan associations, and master and collective trusts. Besides meeting the securities requirement, banks and savings and loan associations must have net worth of at least $25 million. In contrast to other institutional investors, broker-dealers must own only $10 million of securities to qualify as a QIB. Moreover, if acting solely as an agent or a riskless principal, a broker-dealer does not have to be a QIB to place the securities.

The legal underpinning that the SEC used for Rule 144A is from the legislative history of the Securities Act. The SEC concluded that the Congress never considered sophisticated institutional investors to need the protection offered by the registration of securities. Rather, the purpose of registration was to protect unsophisticated, individual investors. Thus, transactions in private placements involving only institutional investors may be legally separated from those involving individual investors. The implication of this argument, as embodied in Rule 144A, is that by establishing a class of private placement transactions confined solely to a well-defined class of sophisticated institutional investors, such transactions would be exempt from registration because they do not constitute an offering to the public. In essence, QIBs are not considered part of the public; therefore, sales to them involve no public offering, and sellers are not considered to be underwriters. QIBs can thus rely on section 4(1) of the Securities Act, which exempts secondary transactions not involving a dealer, underwriter, or issuer, and dealers can rely on section 4(3), which exempts transactions conducted as a part of dealer market making (SEC, 1988).

Underwriting of Private Placements

The dealer exemption indirectly carries with it the authority to underwrite new issues of private placements. Generally speaking, an underwriting occurs when an investment bank purchases securities from the issuer with a view to reselling or distributing those securities to other parties.

Under Rule 144A, as long as the resales are to QIBs, the activity is interpreted not as an under- writing or distribution but rather as a secondary market transaction. Consequently, an issuer may sell the securities to an "underwriter" using section 4(2) or Regulation D for an exemption from registration, and the underwriter may then resell the securities to eligible institutional investors relying on Rule 144A.

When a Rule 144A exemption is available, the buyer does not need to provide a letter stating that the purchase of the securities is for investment purposes, as it does with a traditional private placement. Rather, the buyer supplies information confirming its eligibility to purchase the securities under Rule 144A. The buyer also must agree not to resell the securities without having an exemption (Weigley, 1991).

SEC's Reasons for Adopting Rule 144A

The SEC adopted Rule 144A for three reasons (SEC, 1988). One was to formalize market practice regarding resales of private placements by eliminating the uncertainty surrounding the use of the section 4(11/2) exemption. A second was to increase the liquidity of private placements.

Although a significant volume of trading that relied upon the section 4(11/2) exemption and Rule 144 had ocurred during the 1980s, most market participants felt that the conditions of those exemptions resulted in reduced liquidity in the primary and secondary markets.

Finally, the SEC hoped that Rule 144A would make the private placement market more attractive to foreign corporations. The SEC was motivated in part by the growing desire of many U.S. investors to purchase foreign securities in the United States without incurring the costs of obtaining them in foreign markets. Even though U.S. markets offered many advantages to foreign issuers—including a broad investor base, the opportunity to diversify funding sources, virtually the only source of long-term, fixed-rate funds, and financing for non-investment-grade companies—foreign corporations had not been a significant presence in U.S. markets, and thus their securities were not readily available to domestic investors.

Foreign corporations are reluctant to issue in the public and private markets for several reasons. In the public market, they are discouraged by the expense and the time involved in registering the securities with the SEC and in satisfying the continuing requirements for reporting. Particularly burdensome in this regard is the requirement that financial statements conform to U.S. generally accepted accounting principles. Some potential issuers are also loathing to disclose more information about their operations than that required in their home countries. Finally, the potential for litigation, brought by either the SEC or investors, that accompanies registration is a significant deterrent for many foreign corporations (Engros, 1992; Gurwitz, 1990).

Despite appearances, the burden of registration and disclosure requirements may not be as great as perceived by many potential foreign issuers. For example, relative to domestic issuers, the SEC requires much less disclosure for foreign corporations with limited business interests in the United States or limited ownership by U.S. residents, although the financial statements must, in part, still be reconciled with U.S. generally accepted accounting principles. Also, if shares of a foreign corporation are not listed on a U.S. stock exchange or quoted on the NASDAQ system, the SEC requires under Rule 12g3-2(b) only that the corporation provide information made public in its home country. 176 Nevertheless, outsiders have held the view that the disclosure requirements associated with public offerings in the United States are burdensome.

Although privately placed securities are a means for foreign corporations to avoid registration and public disclosure altogether, prior to adoption of Rule 144A foreign corporations had not issued extensively in the private market either. This was partly the result of the higher yields of traditional private placements. In addition, the greater frequency of restrictive covenants in private placements than found in securities issued in foreign markets and the negotiation of terms caused many potential issuers to shy away from the private market.

In adopting Rule 144A, the SEC hoped to lower one of the barriers to foreign issuance caused by the illiquidity of private placements. Also, by adopting Regulation S at the same time as Rule 144A, the SEC facilitated sales of overseas offerings by foreign and U.S. issuers in the private placement market. Regulation S stipulates conditions under which offshore offerings and resales of securities, whether issued by U.S. corporations or by foreign entities, are not required to be registered with the SEC. Generally, as long as securities transactions take place outside the United States and no effort is directed toward selling to persons within the United States, offshore transactions are exempt from registration with the SEC. Under Regulation S, selling activities involved in the distribution of private placements and in resales pursuant to Rule 144A are not considered to be directed selling efforts. Thus, in contemporaneous offerings of securities inside and outside the United States, for which the securities sold in the United States are privately placed, the exemption from registration provided by Regulation S is preserved. Moreover, in strictly offshore offerings, Regulation S generally allows securities to be sold in the United States to QIBs without registration (SEC, 1990b; Morison, 1990). Taken together, Rule 144A and Regulation S have thus eased the way for foreign corporations engaged in offshore offerings to enter the 144A market.

The Market for Privately Placed Equity Securities

The private placement market for corporate equity securities consists of all equity securities not registered with the Securities and Exchange Commission. The private equity market overlaps to some extent with that segment of the private debt market that includes debt with equity kickers; indeed, private market participants specializing in the debt or equity side often view this segment as part of "their" market. For this study, however, we have included bonds with equity kickers as part of the debt market. Even so, the private equity market consists of a wide range of financings—straight equity, venture capital, and equity for mergers and acquisitions—funded by a variety of investors.

Apart from the type of security, the private debt and equity markets differ in several other respects. Insurance companies do not dominate the private equity market as they do the market for privately placed debt. State and large corporate pension funds, endowment funds, finance companies, corporations, and individual investors are all important sources of funds in the private equity market. In addition, the average annual volume of issuance of private debt substantially exceeds that of private equity. Finally, a large amount of financing in the equity market is conducted through private limited partnerships.

Recent Trends in Issuance

Gross issuance of private equity is a fraction of that of private debt. Since peaking in 1989, total issuance of privately placed equity has fallen considerably. However, the dollar volume of private equity financing, even at its peak, was less than 25 percent of that in the private debt market.

Much of the recent decline in private equity issuance reflects changes in the activity of limited partnerships, which raise funds through the sale of partnership interests and make equity investments in companies. Sales of these interests, which are themselves treated as private placements, appear to make up the bulk of gross issuance by the financial sector. In 1990, for example, almost 90 per- cent of total financial sector issuance was in the other financial category, which is dominated by limited-partnership investment funds. The volume of limited-partnership issuance appears to be particularly sensitive to the pace of merger activity in the economy. The sharp decline in mergers and acquisitions in 1991 was reflected in the dramatic decrease in issuance by the other financial sector from $9.4 billion in 1990 to $2.6 billion in 1991.

The relative sizes of gross issuance in the public and private equity markets since 1986 for nonfinancial firms. Until 1991, when firms issued unprecedented amounts of new public equity, the private market made up a healthy share of total gross equity financing by U.S. firms. One reason for the 1991 decline may have been the very high price-earnings ratios in the public market that siphoned issuance from the private market. Indeed, movement on the margin between the public and the private equity markets by smaller firms is likely to be much greater than that between the public and the private debt markets; whereas few public debt issues are for less than $100 million, many public equity offerings are.

Another reason for the 1991 decline may have been the further slowing of merger and acquisition activity among firms. Although firms may have pared their acquisition plans in 1991 in response to the recession, the reluctance of domestic banks to provide senior loans for merger deals may also have contributed to the lower volume of equity issuance by smaller firms. Also, insurance companies cut back their investments in the private equity market in 1991. Market participants note, however, that pension funds, some foreign banks, and a few finance companies may have somewhat stepped up their presence in the market.

Investors, Issuers, and Terms of Issuance

Twenty to thirty years ago, life insurance companies were the major buyers in the private equity market. Not only did they invest directly in companies themselves, they also provided the lion's share of the funds for the limited partner- ships, which first appeared in the early 1970s.

These investment funds raise capital from institutional investors and provide private equity financing. The funds target small firms with growth potential that, at their current stage of development, are shut out of the public equity market.

The funds typically have a life of five to ten years; at dissolution, the general partners (the managers of the fund) take their cut, and the remaining returns are distributed to the limited partners (the contributing investors). These funds have grown in number and size over the past twenty years.

Since 1989, however, the major sources of finance in the market have been corporate and state pension funds. The pension funds invest primarily through limited partnerships as they do not have the expertise to invest directly in companies themselves. Market participants estimate that pension funds now provide more than half of all financing for the partnership funds. Finance companies, endowment funds, corporate investors, and individuals provide the rest. In the early 1990s, insurance companies were only minor contributors of new capital to the market, no doubt because of their reallocation of funds toward less- risky borrowers in all markets, including the private debt market.

The structure of private equity investments can vary significantly, from simple common stock to preferred stock with a plethora of restrictive features that allow investors to maintain control over the company's direction. Such features typically include the right to elect directors, voting rights for major transactions contemplated by management, antidilution protection, and Board control at the option of investors if certain performance criteria are not met. Market participants expect more complex forms of equity securities to evolve in response to the growth of more specialized partnership funds.

Typical issuers in the market include those firms too small to tap the public markets for financing. Large troubled companies also often look to the private market to obtain equity infusions from financial institutions or wealthy individuals that would be hard to obtain in a widely distributed public offering. In 1991, for example, Manufacturers Hanover and Citicorp raised a total of $1.5 billion in private offerings of preferred stock. In February 1992,

Chrysler raised $400 million of equity in a private offering.

The traditional forms of "exit" for the private equity investor are either an initial public offering (IPO) or the sale of the company to another (typically corporate) investor. The IPO has been particularly popular in the past couple of years as investors in the public equity market have been very receptive to private companies seeking initial public equity. Market participants also point to the future possibility of selling private equity securities in the secondary market, should that market become sufficiently liquid. Here some disagreement has arisen over the potential effect of Rule 144A. Some feel that the rule will eventually increase liquidity in the secondary market, whereas others feel that it has merely formalized prevailing market practice and consequently will not significantly affect the market. There is general agreement, however, that the market will become more liquid over time—with or without Rule 144A—simply because increasing participation of pension funds in the market will expand the amount of funds invested in equity private placements.

Market participants feel that the share of financing from pension funds could easily grow to 70 or 75 percent and that this growth could be a major factor in the growth of the share of private equity financing that limited- partnership funds provide. They also expect, however, that some large corporate pension funds and some insurance companies will continue to invest directly in companies. Pension funds may be willing to allocate increasing shares of their portfolios to the private equity market for several reasons. First, the private market offers the opportunity to diversify assets outside the traditional public stock and bond markets. Second, to the extent that the private market is less efficient than its public counterpart, it offers investors the chance to make superior returns. Finally, by placing funds with active investors (the limited partnerships) that take controlling positions in companies and monitor and sometimes change management, pension funds can participate in the increased returns generated by the turning around of poorly managed companies.

Legal and Regulatory Restrictions on Bank Participation in the Private Placement Market

Commercial banks may participate in the private placement market as issuers, buyers, agents, and brokers, but they are subject to legal and regulatory restrictions in some of these activities.

Banks as Issuers

No restrictions on issuance of privately placed securities apply specifically to commercial banks or bank holding companies. Like other issuers, these entities must comply with securities laws.

Summary of Bank Powers To Buy Private Placements

we summarize bank powers to buy private placements, which vary with the nature of the security and the type of buyer. Briefly, and ignoring exceptions detailed below, banks may not buy privately placed equity, but they may buy private debt, so long as it is booked for regulatory purposes as a loan. Bank holding companies may buy limited amounts of equity and may buy privately placed debt without restriction.

Bank Purchases of Privately Placed Debt

Two complexities prevent a simple yes-or-no answer to the question "May banks buy privately placed debt for their own accounts?" First, regulatory authority over banks operating in the United States is divided. National banks are regulated primarily by the Office of the Comptroller of the Currency (OCC), state-chartered banks that are members of the Federal Reserve System and foreign banks are regulated by the Federal Reserve, and state-chartered nonmember banks (with FDIC insurance) by the FDIC. State-chartered banks must also comply with restrictions imposed by state authorities.

The second complication is that financial instruments that are securities for some legal and regulatory purposes may be loans for other legal and regulatory purposes.

National bank activities involving securities are subject to the Glass-Steagal Act (12 USC § 24(7)) and to the investment securities regulation of the OCC (12 CFR Part 1). Glass-Steagal specifically authorizes national banks to purchase for their own account "investment securities," which the OCC defines to be "a marketable obligation in the form of a bond, note, or debenture which is commonly regarded as an investment security. [They are not] investments which are predominantly speculative in nature." 179 To date, the OCC has taken the position that private placements are not "marketable" (because of the absence of a public market for such securities), and thus such securities are not eligible for purchase as "investment securities" by national banks. 180 However, they may be purchased and classified as loans for regulatory purposes, so long as normal loan underwriting procedures are followed. That is, private placements may be booked as loans so long as the creditworthiness of the borrower (issuer) is evaluated and documented.

Regulatory treatment of securities as loans is not unusual. Banks have long been permitted to classify as loans their purchases of commercial paper, which is commonly recognized as a security. The OCC has explicitly stated that the classification of an instrument as a security for the purposes of securities law does not necessarily mean it must be a security for purposes of banking law.

The Federal Reserve Act makes state-chartered member banks subject to Glass-Steagal restrictions on securities activities. 183 The Federal Reserve's practice has to date generally followed that of the OCC in matters of investment security regulation. 184 Thus state- chartered member banks also may not book private placements as investment securities, but they may classify private placements as loans if proper underwriting procedures are followed. In the same vein as OCC writings on this subject, the Federal Reserve Board's

Commercial Bank Examination Manual states:

Occasionally, examiners will have difficulty distinguishing between a loan and a security. Loans result from direct negotiations between a borrower and a lender.

A bank will refuse to grant a loan unless the borrower agrees to its terms. A security, on the other hand, is usually acquired through a third party, a broker or dealer in securities. Most securities have standardized terms which can be compared to the terms of other market offerings. Because the terms of most loans do not lend themselves to such comparison, the average investor may not accept the terms of the lending arrangement. Thus, an individual loan cannot be regarded as a readily marketable security.

The securities investments of state nonmember banks are subject to the restrictions of relevant state laws, rather than to those of the Glass- Steagal Act. Banks with FDIC deposit insurance (that is, almost all banks) are also subject to FDIC regulations. The FDIC has generally followed OCC practice in this area, with one possible exception, but recent legislation may lead to some departure from OCC practice. A recent amendment to the FDI Act (12 USC 1831a), which was part of the FDIC Improvement Act (FDICIA), prohibits any insured state bank from engaging as principal in any activity that is not permissible for a national bank unless the state bank meets its capital requirements and the FDIC consents. Since "activity" includes making any investment, an insured state bank is now able to ask the FDIC for permission to place in its investment account debt securities that do not qualify as investment securities.

The other possible departure from OCC practice involves the fact that some states grant banks authority to make "leeway" investments, that is, to buy limited quantities of certain securities that are otherwise ineligible. Except for securities in default, the FDIC will not criticize such investments so long as they are permitted by applicable state law, the total of all such investments does not exceed 10 percent of equity capital and surplus, and the investments have been approved by the bank's board of directors or trustees as leeway securities.

The types of securities that qualify as leeway securities vary by state, but those acceptable to the FDIC as leeway investments are limited mainly to securities that state or local governments issue or guarantee, some of which may also qualify as private placements. We speculate that if any private placements of debt have been purchased by banks under this authority, the quantity has been insignificant.

The distinction between buying a private placement for an investment security account and a loan account has little economic meaning. Since due diligence similar to that in commercial loan underwriting is the norm in the private placement market, in practice commercial banks appear not to be generally restricted from purchasing private placements. One perhaps unintended effect of current regulations is possible, however. Some private placement agents have in recent years developed distribution channels that employ public security sales forces. These channels are most often used for the placements, especially Rule 144A placements, of highly rated or well-known borrowers. Some of these channels circumscribe the ability of buyers to perform the in-depth due diligence that is normal for traditional private placements. Under current regulations, banks may be restricted from buying such placements because they may be unable to provide the underwriting documentation necessary to their classification as loans. If such restriction actually occurs, current regulations will unintentionally discourage bank investments in some higher-quality and more-liquid private placements and permit the purchase of riskier and less- liquid placements.

Bank Purchases of Privately Placed Equity

To a first approximation, national and state member banks may not purchase equity for their own accounts.

The exceptions are numerous, however. Those for state member banks (regulated by the Federal Reserve) are detailed in table C.2, which is a copy of table 1 in section 203.1 of the Board's Commercial Bank Examination Manual. The manner of issue of the equity securities, public or private, is immaterial.

FDICIA extended the Glass-Steagal limitations on equity investments to state-chartered nonmember banks: Insured state banks are now generally prohibited from acquiring or retaining any equity security that is not permissible for a national bank. Some exceptions exist, however, for certain kinds of equity investments and for banks that had made such investments during a given period, provided that the FDIC does not object and a capital limitation is not breached.

Bank Holding Company Purchases of Privately Placed Debt and Equity

Bank holding companies, which are regulated by the Federal Reserve Board under the Bank Holding Company Act of 1956, may purchase debt securities, whether publicly issued or privately placed. Regulation of equity purchases also does not regard the manner of issuance. Holding companies may purchase up to 5 percent of the voting stock of any nonbank corporation without prior Board approval, though such investments must be passive. They may purchase up to 24.9 percent of a nonbank firm's total capital, including subordinated debt and nonvoting stock; again, the investment must be passive.

Banks as Agents

Current law and regulation allow banks to act as agents for issuers of private placements, but restrictions on their activities differ somewhat depending on whether the activity is performed in a bank, in a securities affiliate of a bank holding company (section 20 subsidiary), or in another nonbank subsidiary of a bank holding company. Fein (1991) discusses the legal history of bank securities powers, which involved legal challenges by the Securities Industry Association and others.

Agent activities have few restrictions when they are performed in a bank. 190 A bank need not obtain permission to act as an agent. However, it should structure its relationships with issuers so that it acts as adviser (without power to commit the issuer formally) rather than as agent (with such power). (In this study, the word agent refers to both agents and advisers.) Issues for which national and state-chartered member banks act as agent may be placed in the bank's own accounts, in trust accounts or other managed accounts, or with other affiliates or the parent holding company (if these exist). A bank's main obligation, and the main focus of examinations of bank private placement agent activities, is to fully disclose information about the bank's interests to all parties involved in a transaction.

This disclosure permits parties to assess the risk flowing from any potential conflicts of interest on the part of the bank. In particular, but not exclusively, the bank must disclose any lending relationships with issuers or with potential or actual buyers of the securities

Terms of Privately Placed Debt Contracts

Private placements generally have fixed interest rates, intermediate-to long-term maturities, and moderately large issue sizes. Their contracts frequently include restrictive covenants. These terms differ from those found in other markets for debt, for example, the markets for bank loans and publicly issued bonds.

Issue Size

On average, private placements are larger than bank loans and smaller than public bonds. In 1989, the median new commercial and industrial (C&I) bank loan was for about $50,000; more than 96 percent were less than $10 million. When loan size distributions were computed by volume rather than number, large loans naturally accounted for a larger share. The mean loan size was about $1 million. The 3.6 percent of loans for $10 million or more accounted for 58 percent of total loan volume. Although most are small, loans for as much as $100 million are not extraordinary.

In contrast, the median private placement issued by nonfinancial corporations in 1989 was $32 million, and the mean was $76 million. None was less than $250,000 (compared with 70 percent of bank loans in that category). Most private placements were for amounts between $10 million and $100 million. The median public issue was $150 million, and the mean public issue was $181 million. Most public issues were larger than $100 million. None was smaller than $10 million, and only 15 percent were smaller than $100 million.

In interviews, market participants often remarked that the private market is cost-effective mainly for issues larger than $10 million, whereas the public market is cost-effective for issues larger than $100 million. The data are consistent with this assertion, as only 10 percent to 15 percent of private placements and underwritten public issues (excluding medium-term note issues) fall below the respective boundaries.

These cross-market patterns in size of financing are often attributed to economies of scale in issue size, that is, to declining costs to the issuer, including fees and interest costs, as issue size increases. Such arguments are usually based on a perception that, holding all else constant, interest rates are lowest in the public market and highest in the bank loan market and on a perception that fixed costs of issuance are highest in the public market, smaller in the private market, and lowest in the bank loan market.

An alternative, possibly overlapping explanation is that the three markets specialize in providing different kinds of financing to different kinds of borrowers and that relevant borrower characteristics are associated with issue size. In particular, borrowers of large amounts are often big and well-established firms that require relatively little initial due diligence and loan monitoring by lenders, whereas those borrowing small amounts often require much due diligence and monitoring. Thus, borrowers of small-to-moderate

SIR PATRICK BIJOU

amounts usually must borrow in the private placement or bank loan markets, where lenders are organized to serve information-problematic borrowers, whereas those borrowing larger amounts usually can issue in the public market because they are not information problematic. As we show later in part 1, both explanations are important, but the second explanation is probably more important in determining the market in which a borrower issues debt.

Maturity and Prepayment Penalties

According to their maturity distributions, commercial and industrial bank loans tend to have relatively short maturities, private placements tend to have intermediate- to long-term maturities, and public bonds have the highest proportion of long maturities. In 1989, the median bank loan had a maturity of just over three months, and the mean maturity was around nine months 18 Almost 80 percent of loans had maturities of less than one year. When weighted by loan size, two-thirds of loans had maturities shorter than one month. In interviews, market participants often stated that banks seldom lend long term, even when the loan interest rate floats. They stated that loans in the three- to five-year range are not uncommon, five- to seven-year loans are less common, and loans longer than seven years are rare. These remarks are supported by the charts.

The distributions in the charts are for a nonrandom sample of new loans, not for loans on the and the nature of any compensation it will receive for assisting the transaction.

Bank holding companies wishing to serve as agents of private placements either in the holding company or in a nonbank affiliate must first obtain the Board's permission. When it is so located, the activity is subject to additional restrictions

- An issue may be placed with nonbank affiliates only up to 50 percent of the amount of the placement, and no issue may be placed with bank affiliates.
- Loans that are the functional equivalents of purchasing for the account of an affiliate and loans to cover unsold portions of an issue cannot be and the nature of any compensation it will receive for assisting the transaction.

Bank holding companies wishing to serve as agents of private placements either in the holding company or in a nonbank affiliate must first obtain the Board's permission. When it is so located, the activity is subject to additional restrictions made to issuers.

Holding companies must be able to document that any credit to an issuer was extended under different terms, for different purposes, and at different times than were the securities being placed.

- Loans cannot be made to the issuer to cover principal and interest payments until at least three years have passed since issuance.

- Issues may not be placed with accounts managed by affiliated bank trust departments nor with other accounts advised or managed by affiliates.

- No lines of credit or other guarantees may be provided to support privately placed issues advised by the affiliate. For example, no affiliate of the holding company may provide a backup line of credit to support a placement of commercial paper advised by a nonbank affiliate.

- The notes for an issue must be in denominations of at least $100,000.

- All lending relationships of the consolidated holding company with the issuer must be disclosed to actual and potential purchasers, and no investment advice may be provided to purchasers.

- Securities may be placed only with accredited investors.

- The securities may not be registered.

- The issue must comply with relevant securities laws, for example, there can be no public solicitation nor offering.

- When acting as agent for a private placement, section 20 subsidiaries must comply with some additional restrictions that apply to public under¬writings. Non-section 20 subsidiaries need not do so.

Several foreign banks have received permission to conduct agent activities in securities subsidiaries, subject to the above restrictions, some details of which differ because of the banks. foreign status. U.S. branches of foreign banks and U.S. banks owned by foreign banks may also act as agents in the private market, in which case they are subject to the regulations of the relevant bank regulator.

These restrictions are more stringent than those faced by banks. For example, in its No Objection Letter 87-3 (March 24, 1987) and its Interpretive Letter 496 (December 18, 1989), the OCC permitted banks to act as agents in the private placement of registered securities of their holding companies or subsidiaries. Banks may provide lines of credit to issuers they advise and may place advised issues with affiliates and in trust or managed accounts, subject to guidance from regulators.

Bank Activities in the Secondary Market for Private Placements

In general, banks and non-section 20 subsidiaries may act as traders of securities, regardless of the nature of their issuance, but not as brokers or dealers. Section 20 subsidiaries may act as brokers or dealers. In practice, the ability of banks to actively trade private placements is limited because such placements must be booked as loans (as noted above) and normal loan underwriting standards apply. The requirement that analyses of creditworthiness be performed may not be a substantial hindrance in the secondary market for traditional private placements, in which most buyers intend to hold purchases for some time and for which due diligence is the norm. However, extensive credit analyses are more unusual in the Rule 144A secondary market, which operates much like the public bond market. Thus, except for section 20 subsidiaries, banks may have difficulty participating in this market.

CHAPTER 9

A Review of the Empirical Evidence on Covenants and Renegotiation

The Nature of Covenants in Private Placements

Laber (1992) has examined the frequency of different types of covenants in private placements. From a sample of twenty-five private placements issued between 1989 and mid-1991, he found that all had covenants that (1) related to mergers and consolidations, (2) restricted the sale of assets, (3) restricted liens given to other creditors, and (4) restricted either payments (dividends, stock repurchases, and payments to preferred stock) or net worth. Eighty-eight percent had covenants that set a maximum leverage ratio; 72 percent had covenant that restricted investments; and 48 percent had covenants that required a minimum interest coverage ratio. Laber did not report on the frequency of covenants related to working capital, although such covenants do appear in private placements.

According to market participants, most financial covenants in private placements are incurrence covenants; occasionally one or two maintenance covenants may be included, especially when these are designed to match maintenance covenants in other debt of the issuer, such as bank loans.

The Relationship between Covenant Tightness and Issuer Quality

Our discussion with market participants indicated that the number and tightness of financial covenants in private placements, just as in other debt markets, are a function of the quality of the issuer. Securities purchase agreements for lower-quality issuers often include many of the financial covenants seen by Laber, and the covenants are tight in that stipulated minimum values for ratios are close to current values. Contracts for moderately risky issuers often include only one or two financial covenants with minimum values set further from current values. Highly rated issues usually have no financial covenants, although A-rated issues may have a debt-incurrence covenant if their maturity is beyond seven years.

In contrast, Hawkins (1982) found in a sample of fifty securities issued in the mid-1970s no relationship between the restrictiveness of covenants in private placements and the quality of the issuer, for three types of financial covenants: working capital restrictions, cash payout restrictions, and debt restrictions. One reason for Hawkins's findings is that the market may have changed in the 1980s. Indeed, many observers have argued that covenants in private placements have become less restrictive over the past decade (Asquith and Wizman, 1990; Brealey and Myers, 1991; Brook, 1990; and McDaniel, 1988). If restrictiveness has decreased more for higher-quality issues than for lower-quality issues, then the difference would be accounted for. Along this line, Asquith and Wizman found for public bonds that covenant restrictions on debt financing and dividends fell more for A-rated bonds than for lower-rated bonds. Fitch (1991), however, states that the decline in the strength of public bond indentures is characteristic of the public market and not the private placement market. The decline is also inconsistent with the interview results of Brook (1990) and the market descriptions of Chemical Bank (1992) and Travelers Insurance Company (1992).

Cross-Market Differences in Covenants

Market participants indicated that bank loans contain roughly the same types of covenants as those in the private placement market, with two differences. First, financial covenants in bank loans are typically maintenance covenants, whereas most covenants in private placements are incurrence covenants. Second, bank loan covenants are usually tighter. In some cases, we were informed, private placement covenants are set by loosening the covenants in an issuer's existing bank loan.

Although the types of financial covenants are roughly the same in private placements and bank loans, evidence points to subtle differences in the way they are implemented. Travelers (1992) observes that bank loan covenants tend to reflect a lending philosophy different from that motivating private placement covenants. It argues that banks, as short-term lenders, emphasize liquidity or working capital. This approach is reflected in the inclusion of working capital covenants. Banks also appear to be more sensitive to the relation between total liabilities and net worth; therefore, bank loans tend to restrict the ratio of total liabilities to net worth. In contrast, private placement investors tend to emphasize the importance of a firm's long-term assets and its long-term debt because they are long-term investors. As a result, according to Travelers (1992), private placements seldom include working capital covenants, and they tend to restrict long-term liabilities rather than total liabilities.

Empirical Evidence on Cross-Market Differences

Several studies that focused on the differences between covenants in privately placed debt and those in public debt indicate that private placement covenants are tighter than public bond covenants.

Smith and Warner (1979) observed this fact from a 1971 American Bar Foundation study of bond indentures. Laber's (1992) conclusion that covenants in the private placement market are more restrictive than those in the public market was based on a comparison of his private placement data with the findings of other studies of covenants in the public market. DeAngelo, DeAngelo, and Skinner (1990) also presented evidence that the covenants of private debt contracts are tighter than those of public debt contracts. El-Gazzar and Pastena (1990) had similar results and also reported that private placement covenants tend to be tighter than those in large syndicated bank loans. This finding, however, probably reflects the predominance of large syndicated bank facilities in their sample as opposed to loans to the smaller bank-dependent borrowers that are the focus of our comparison. 195 Because they did not appropriately control for issuer size and quality in their analysis, their results are not inconsistent with the general proposition that bank loan covenants associated with bank- dependent borrowers are tighter than private placement covenants, which are in turn tighter than public bond covenants, controlling for the size and quality of the borrower.

From interviews with staff of investment banks, rating agencies, corporate general counsel departments, and law firms, Brook (1990) found that private placements typically had tighter covenants than public bonds had but that the pattern differed by type of covenant For three classes of covenants—disposition of assets or maintenance of capital, limitations on debt, and restrictions on dividends—private placements were the most restrictive, non-investment-grade public bonds were somewhat less restrictive, and investment-grade public bonds were the least restrictive.

Brook also found that restrictions on investments were not present in public bonds but were common in private placements. However, negative pledge clauses and restrictions on sale-leaseback transactions were common to all three. 196 Anti- merger provisions were present in all three types of securities. Some interviewees in the Brook study, however, indicated that antimerger covenants tended to be somewhat stronger in the non-investment-grade market and stronger yet in the private market. He found that in the public bond market the typical anti-merger provision did not prevent a merger but only required that the acquirer assume the acquiree's debt.

The Value of Covenant Protection

Another empirical issue is the value of covenant protection. Unfortunately, data limitations and the lack of market prices make examination of this issue problematic for the bank loan and the private placement markets. However, several studies have been conducted on the degree of protection provided by covenants in public bonds for leveraged buyouts. These studies focus on the relation between covenants and bondholder returns in leveraged buyouts (LBOs). (A loss, or negative return, to existing bondholders due to an LBO indicates a lack of covenant protection.) Marais, Schipper, and Smith (1989) found that existing bondholders did not suffer losses in LBOs.

However, their results contrast with anecdotal evidence, such as the RJR-Nabisco leveraged buyout, as well as other academic studies, such as Warga and

Welch (1990). Asquith and Wizman's (1990) results are particularly relevant: They found that, although existing bondholders on average incurred significant losses in LBOs, these losses were related to the strength of the covenants. They found that "bonds with strong covenant protection gain value, whereas those with weak or no protection lose value." Similar results were obtained by Cook, Easterwood, and Martin (1992). Crabbe (1991b) analyzed the value of covenants in the public market ex ante by examining the pricing of super poison puts. 197 He found that public bonds with super poison put covenants paid a lower yield than those without. It is difficult, however, to extrapolate from these studies of the value of event risk protection in the public market to the value of credit quality protection provided by covenants in the private market. Of course, the ubiquity of covenants in private placements and commercial bank loans itself suggests that they are valued in these markets.

Empirical Evidence on Renegotiation

While virtually all sources, including market participants interviewed for this study, agree on the ranking of markets with respect to covenant tightness and renegotiation, some evidence suggests that public bond covenants can provide a measure of protection and that the cost of renegotiation in the public market is not necessarily prohibitive. Kahan and Tuckman (1992) studied covenant renegotiation in public bonds. They found a sample of sixty-nine firms that sought to renegotiate bond covenants during 1988 and 1989. The authors argue that their finding so many firms seeking renegotiation is inconsistent with the assumption of most researchers (for example, Berlin and Loeys, 1988; Bulow and Shoven, 1978; and Lummer and McConnell, 1989) that renegotiation is limited to the information¬intensive markets (for example, commercial bank loans and private placements) and is prohibitively expensive in the public market. Covenant renegotiation in the public bond market involves the issuer's sending a "consent solicitation" to each bondholder requesting an alteration in one or more of the covenants in the bond indenture agreement. Except for an alteration of interest and principal provisions, most indenture agreements require a two-thirds majority of the outstanding face value of the bond issue. (The T rust Indenture Act of 1939 requires the consent of all bondholders when principal and interest are to be modified.) Kahan and Tuckman (1992) found that most solicitations are ultimately successful but noted that many of the solicitations have a coercive element in that the consenting bondholders receive a fee (typically $10 per $1,000 of face value) if the solicitation is successful, whereas those not consenting receive no fee. They also found, however, that bondholders enjoyed, on average, significant positive abnormal returns around the announcement of "potentially" coercive solicitations. This finding suggests that issuing firms "cannot, or do not, exploit the coercive nature of their solicitations."

The evidence presented by Asquith and Wizman (1990) and Kahan and Tuckman (1992) may appear inconsistent with the view that covenants are not binding in the public market, but it is not necessarily so. The results in both of these studies were driven by extraordinary events. In the Asquith and Wizman study, the events were LBOs. Similarly, the largest category by far in the Kahan and Tuckman sample also involved firms that were targets of an LBO (and most others involved relatively unusual events). The results of these studies suggest that covenants in public bonds can impose meaningful limitations on event risk. When more routine types of actions by firms are likely to trigger bank or private placement covenants, however, public bond covenants are normally not binding. In a sample of 128 firms that violated accounting-based covenants, Chen, and Wei (1991) found that only 4 involved public debt. The remainder were privately placed securities.

An Example of a Private Placement Assisted by an Agent

In late spring 1991, Acme Stores, Inc., opened negotiations with its primary bank, BigBank, to renew a revolving credit agreement that had been in force for three years. Acme Stores is a publicly held company with $1 billion in annual sales, operating in a highly competitive area of the retail sales sector. BigBank is a bank affiliate of a large U.S. bank holding company.

The occasion inspired wide-ranging discussions between officers of Acme and those of BigBank about Acme's current and prospective capital needs. BigBank's officers adopted the "corporate finance" perspective now coming into fashion among loan officers at many of the large banks, in which the loan officer advises on financial strategies involving a wide range of instruments instead of focusing on the sale of bank loans. BigBank noted that the history of takedowns and repayments for the existing revolver indicated that about $30 million of the $45 million now outstanding was essentially a term loan that probably would not be repaid in the near future. Traditionally, BigBank noted, an expiring revolver would have been rolled over into a combination of a term loan for the longer-term component of the balance and a line of credit for the remaining, seasonal component. BigBank was not devoted to tradition and said that it would be happy to arrange a new revolver if that was desired, as Acme was a relatively high-quality borrower. BigBank stated, however, that investors often look more favorably on middle-market companies that have obtained long-term debt financing and that this point in the interest cycle appeared to be a good time to borrow at a fixed rate.

Acme was interested in obtaining long-term, fixed-rate financing. BigBank noted that a floating- rate term loan could be swapped into fixed rate, but the maximum maturity that BigBank could offer would be about five years. Acme was in principle interested in a longer term. BigBank advised that the combination of Acme's size, business profile, financial condition, and the amount of the term loan (around $30 million) was such that a public offering of debt was infeasible but that a private placement including some financial covenants might be an attractive option. At this point, BigBank's private placement agent was called in for consultation. As a major corporate lender, BigBank had found setting up its own private placement agent organization profitable.

Based on a quick review of Acme and its financial position, the agent estimated that a private placement of fixed-rate, senior, unsecured notes with a maturity of about ten years would be feasible. Current private market conditions for borrowers like Acme were such that the loan would have to amortize; a bullet loan probably could not be placed with investors. Further discussion yielded a plan for an issue of $32 million of eight-year notes, with annual principal repayments of $4 million.

The agent explained the best-efforts nature of the process. In cooperation with Acme, BigBank would design an initial set of terms for the securities and then seek investors, which would likely be life insurance companies. BigBank would not guarantee the pricing of the issue. Terms might change during negotiations with the investors, and the possibility of no deal being struck was real. BigBank's fee would be 3/4 of 1 percent of the face amount of the placement, but the fee would be collected only if the placement were successful. After signing an agent agreement with BigBank, obtaining commitments from investors would take about two months, and funds could be disbursed another month or so after that.

Acme sought bids and advice from other private placement agents and found BigBank's fees to be competitive. It also found that some agents were not interested in the transaction. They explained to Acme that $32 million was a relatively small placement, and that the staff time and other fixed costs to do a placement were about the same regardless of a deal's size. Thus, some agents preferred to concentrate only on larger transactions for which the fees were larger.

Acme also knew that it had to renew its revolver before funds from the private placement would be available. If the private placement did not succeed, Acme would need either a term loan or a larger revolver, which would be easiest to negotiate if BigBank were the agent that failed to complete the private placement. Thus Acme gave a mandate to BigBank's agent organization to arrange the transaction.

The agent's first action was to conduct due diligence, meaning it made a close examination of Acme's business, financial position, and plans.

This examination was similar to the one that lenders would later conduct, and it included a visit to Acme's facility. Performance of due diligence was relatively easy for BigBank because its relationship officers already had substantial information about Acme.

Having gathered much information about Acme, the agent began writing the offering memorandum (offer memo) and term sheet. An offer memo describes the borrower and is functionally similar to a prospectus for a public offering. However, it usually includes more information, such as forecasts, than does a prospectus. The term sheet is a description of the major terms of the securities to be offered, including covenants. An interest rate (expressed as a spread over Treasuries of comparable maturity) is generally not included initially. Lenders use the offer memo and term sheet in deciding whether or not to buy the securities.

Initial term sheets vary in their content and detail, depending on the nature and quality of the borrower, the complexity of the transaction, and the distribution style of the agent. In this case, the BigBank agent wrote a relatively detailed term sheet, which included covenants restricting Acme's financial ratios. These covenants were similar to those in the new revolving credit agreement concurrently being negotiated with BigBank. A substantial penalty for prepayment of the note was also included. Although Acme was quite unhappy about this penalty, the agent noted that the securities could not be placed without it. The "final" versions of both the offer memo and term sheet were produced after extensive consultations with Acme, about two weeks after BigBank received the mandate to go ahead.

With the offer memo and term sheet in hand, the agent initiated the process of getting a "pre- rating" of the securities. 202 The NAIC does such ratings only at the request of an insurance company. The agent used a contact to make a request, reimbursing the insurer for the NAIC's fee. This insurance company made no commitment to buy the securities. With securities issued by very-high-quality borrowers, beginning and sometimes even completing distribution with no rating in hand is possible; but with a borderline borrower like Acme and under the market conditions of the time, no lender would seriously consider a purchase without knowing the rating.

The NAIC rating process takes at least three weeks.

Upon obtaining the rating, and finding it to be a NAIC-2 (or BBB) as expected, the agent began looking for investors who would buy the securities. The style in which private placement distributions are conducted varies widely across both agents and transactions. In this case, BigBank's agent noted that the transaction was for a relatively small amount of senior unsecured debt and that the borrower was moderately risky by the standards of the private placement market.

These facts had several implications. First, one or more lead lenders were required. A lead lender is one that commits to buy a significant fraction of the placement and that has the necessary credit evaluation and monitoring capacity to assess the loan's risk, negotiate terms, and monitor performance during the life of the loan. Relatively small lenders with limited evaluation and monitoring capacity will rely to some extent on the quality signal implicit in a lead's commitment when making their own decision to purchase a placement Second, lead buyers of senior unsecured private debt are usually life insurance companies. Third, the largest life insurance companies were less likely to be interested in a transaction of relatively small size.

Thus, BigBank's agent began distributing the placement by sending the term sheet and offer memo to several insurance companies, moderate to large in size, verbally suggesting an interest rate of about 190 basis points over Treasuries. These insurers were known to the agent to be receptive to deals with borrowers in Acme's industry and risk category. 203 The securities were offered to these lenders on a first-come, first-served basis.

Although private market lenders often call the agent to obtain information not in the offer memo, and in rarer cases may perform substantial amounts of independent due diligence before making a commitment, the norm in the private market is for lenders to make semiformal purchase commitments based on analysis of the information in the offer memo and term sheet and to do so fairly rapidly, within a week or two. 204 Potential lead lenders generally indicate interest by making a counteroffer in which they state that they will purchase a given amount at a given rate and with given changes in the other terms.

A life insurance company of moderate size circled (agreed to buy) about half of the placement at a spread of 200 basis points over Treasuries of comparable maturity, and two others followed this lead in committing to another 40 percent or so one at 190 basis points over and one at 195 over Treasuries. Left with only $3 million of notes to place, the agent turned to several smaller insurance companies, offering them all or part of the remaining notes on the terms negotiated with the lead lender. These companies rely most on the signal implicit in the lead lender's decision, as they are offered a take-it-or-leave-it proposition and given only two or three days to decide.

Time required for distribution varies. In this case distribution took about two weeks.

Having fully subscribed the placement, Big- Bank's agent informed the lenders that they were in the syndicate and set the coupon rate (at 200 basis points over Treasuries on that day) and then turned to the next stage, lenders' due diligence. Each of the major lenders conducted an investigation of the borrowing company, including visits to the Acme's facility, that was similar to that done by Bigbank at the beginning of the process. Due diligence is done promptly, and on its completion the lenders' committees pass formal judgment on the loan and dispatch formal commitment letters.

In the final stage of the private issuance, lawyers hammered out the language of the debt contract, which involved several documents besides the notes themselves. The lenders were represented by a bond counsel that was chosen by the lead lender but paid by Acme. Acme was represented by its own counsel with assistance from BigBank. The process of working the contract took three weeks.

Closing ends the process of issuance and the agent's role. In this case, BigBank collected a fee of $240,000. Acme paid down a $30 million bridge portion of its new revolver, which went into effect while the private placement transaction was in progress, and put $2 million into its treasury.

Estimates of Issue-Size and Maturity Distributions

Private Placements

Both issue-size and maturity distributions for new issues of private placements were produced from a database of 1989 private placement issues obtained from IDD Information Services. This firm is associated with the publisher of Investment Dealers' Digest This database includes information about new private issues of both debt and equity, including issue size (amount); issue date; the name of the issuer; the name(s) of the agent(s) involved; the nationality of the issuer; the type of security involved; an industry code for the issuer (an IDD designation, not an SIC code); a maturity date where applicable; an indication of whether the issue was junk, lease-related, or part of an acquisition-related financing; and, in some cases, a coupon rate or a number of shares issued and a few words of descriptive comments. Collected primarily from reports that agents sent to IDD, the data include few or no deals not involving an agent and omit many agent-assisted deals that were unreported. The accuracy of the data has not been verified, and we have reason to believe that at least some of the data are unreliable (for example, the junk designation is usually "no" for issues assisted by Drexel, which does not square with Drexel's reputation for specializing in below-investment-grade issues).

Issue-size distributions were produced using the issue- size (amount) field in the database. Maturity distributions were produced by computing maturity at issue from the issue date and maturity date appearing in the database. This computation often involved some approximation, since in many cases only the month and year (not the day) of issuance and maturity appear in the database, and in some cases only the year of maturity is specified. In these cases, we assumed that the month and day of maturity were the same as the month and day of issuance; in effect, we may have rounded up some maturities to the next year.

Both issue-size and maturity distributions were produced from a sample limited to 1989 issues of bonds by U.S. issuers. Two subsamples were analyzed. The one shown in the text (charts 4, 5, 10, and 11) was for issues by nonfinancial corporate borrowers and excluded medium-term notes, convertible or exchangeable debt, and mortgage-backed securities. This subsample totaled 1,020 issues (maturity dates were available for only 901).

The second subsample excluded only medium- term notes and contained 1,620 issues (maturity dates were available for only 1,373 of them).

The distributions for new issues shown here are not necessarily representative of the distributions for outstanding private placements. Adequate data on outstanding are not available. Kwan and Carleton (1993) report that the average term to maturity for a sample of 563 private placements issued between 1985 and 1992 was 11.12 years, a finding that is in rough agreement with the distributions displayed here.

Publicly Issued Bonds

Issue-size and maturity distributions for new issues of public bonds by U.S. issuers were produced from a sample issued during 1989 by nonfinancial corporations and collected by the Federal Reserve Board from public announcements, proxy statements, and other sources. The subsample analyzed here included no government issues, no medium- term notes, no convertible or exchangeable debt, and no mortgage-backed or other asset-backed securities. An unusual issue related to the RJR-Nabisco merger was also omitted.

Commercial and Industrial Bank Loans

Issue-size and maturity distributions for new or renewed bank loans were produced using data from the Quarterly Survey of Terms of Bank Lending to Business. This survey is of a stratified random sample of approximately 350 banks representing insured commercial banks in the United States. Large banks are oversampled Participating banks report data on all loans to businesses made during the first full week in February, May, August, and November (larger banks report data only for loans made on two or three days of those weeks and only for a subset of branches). Individual survey responses are confidential and include for each loan an amount and maturity date as well as other information. No maturity date is recorded for demand loans with no specific maturity date, and rules for reporting loans made under a revolving credit agreement are complicated, in many cases requiring that no maturity date be reported. Construction and land development loans were omitted from the sample we analyzed.

Several steps were required to arrive at distributions representative of commercial and industrial loans by all banks. First, subsamples of loans by banks reporting for less than five days in a survey week or for less than all branches were blown up to make them comparable to subsamples of five-day, all-branch reporters. Then sample banks were stratified according to size, using them four-quarter averages of total C&I loans outstanding at the end of each quarter (computed from Call Report data). We pooled loans for banks in each stratum and computed size and maturity distributions for each stratum. Essentially, we assumed that the sample of loans made by survey banks in a stratum was representative of the population of 1989 C&I loans made by all banks in that stratum. Distributions were computed for each bank size stratum because loan sizes and loan maturities tend to be related to the size of the lending bank, with larger banks making more large and more long-term loans.

We arrived at loan-size and maturity distributions for all bank loans by taking a weighted average of the distributions for the different bank-size strata. The weighting variables were the fractions of all C&I loans outstanding that all banks in a stratum showed on end- of-quarter Call Reports (averaging these outstandings for all of 1989). That is, having achieved (we hope) representative distributions for each size class of banks (as described in the previous paragraph), we weighted the distributions according to the share of total outstanding loans accounted for by each size class. Because the largest banks make a disproportionate share of C&I loans, the distributions for the large-bank strata had more influence on the final, representative distributions than did the distributions for small-bank strata.

As noted, the distributions are for newly originated or renewed loans, not for the population of loans outstanding. Distributions for outstandings may differ substantially from those for originations, for two principal reasons. First, short-term loans may essentially be overweighted by our method of constructing distributions although a sensitivity analysis indicated that any such overweighting probably has little effect on the estimated distributions. Second, bank loans are often prepaid.

Our distributions have other drawbacks. Most notably, the data available from the survey for revolving credit agreements are limited, and these constitute a significant share of all bank loans.

However, the proper maturity date definition to apply to revolvers in comparing them to private placements and public bonds is not clear.

Here are our top 11 reasons to issue a private placement:

Privacy and Control - Private placements enable companies that value privacy to remain private. In contrast to public debt and equity offerings - which require public filings, disclosures of company information and financing documents and terms - private placement transactions are negotiated confidentially, and public disclosure requirements are limited. With a private placement, companies would not be beholden to public shareholders.

Long Maturities - Private placements provide longer maturities than typical bank financing arrangements. They are ideal for companies seeking to extend or layer their refinancing obligations out beyond the typical 3-5- year bank tenor. Additionally, longer maturities often allow for limited amortization, which can be attractive to companies seeking to invest in capital assets, acquisitions and/or invest in projects that have a longer investment return runway.

Fixed Rate - Typically, private placements are offered at a fixed-interest rate, minimizing interest rate risk. Through a fixed-rate financing, companies can avoid the concern commonly associated with floating-rate coupons, should underlying interest rates rise. A fixed coupon generally allows companies to allocate the cost of debt capital for specific project financings, acquisitions, or large capital investment programs. "Creating capital access in both the private debt and bank markets can allow companies to optimize their access to debt capital."

Diversify Capital Sources - Private placements help diversify a company's sources of capital and capital structure. The stable investment appetite shown by insurance companies and other large institutional investors in the private placement market is typically independent from many of the market variables that impact bank market lending activity. Since the terms of private placements can be customized, these transactions are typically crafted to complement existing bank credit facility capacity as opposed to directly competing with these relationships. Creating capital access in both the private debt and bank markets can allow companies to optimize their access to debt capital. Diversification of financing sources becomes particularly important during market cycles when bank liquidity may be tight.

Additional Capacity - Many companies issue private placements because they have outgrown their borrowing capacity and need capital beyond what their existing lenders (banks, private equity firms, etc.) can provide. Private placements typically focus on cash flow lending metrics and can be completed on either a secured or unsecured basis, depending on the issuer's existing capital structure.

Buy-and-Hold - Private placements are typically "buy-and-hold," meaning the debt investment wouldn't be purchased with the intent to sell to another investor. Thus, private placement borrowers benefit from the ability to create a long-term relationship with the same investor throughout the life of the financing.

Ease of Execution - Private placement financings are regularly completed by both privately-held, middle-market companies as well as large public companies. These transactions provide issuers with access to capital on a scale that rivals underwritten public debt offerings, but without certain preconditional requirements, such as ratings, public registrations, or minimum size restrictions. For public companies, private placements can offer superior execution relative to the public market for small issuance sizes as well as greater structural flexibility.

Cost Savings - A company can often issue a private placement for a much lower all-in cost than it could in a public offering. For public issuers, the Security and Exchange Commission (SEC) related registration, legal documentation and underwriting fees for a public offering can be expensive. Additionally, in contrast to banks that often rely on ancillary services and fee generation to enhance investment return, private placement lenders rely exclusively on the yield from the notes that they purchase. Taking into consideration the yield-equivalent savings on avoided underwriting fees, in conjunction with the yield premium often associated with first time issuers and small issuance premiums, private placements can provide a very attractive alternative to the public debt market. "In many cases, private placements are completed with a single large institutional investor."

Fewer Investors - Unlike issuing securities on the public market, where companies issuing debt securities often deal with hundreds of investors, private placement transactions typically involve fewer than 10-20 investors, and in many cases, are completed with a single large institutional investor. This approach can materially simplify the investor tracking burden for issuers as well as allow them to concentrate their investor-relationship efforts on a few key financial partners.

Familiar Pricing Process - The process for pricing private placements debt transactions is very similar to that of public securities. The coupon set for fixed-rate notes issued reflects the underlying U.S. Treasury rate corresponding to the tenor of the notes issued, plus a credit risk premium (a "credit spread"). This process allows for general transparency as to the approach that institutional investors undertake when establishing the economics of the transaction.

Speed of Execution - The growth and maturity of the private placement market has led to improved standardization of documentation, visibility of pricing and terms as well as increased capacity for financings. As a result, the private market can accommodate transactions as small as $10 million and as large as $1-$2 billion. That, when combined with standardized documentation and a smaller universe of investors, fosters quick execution of an investment, generally within 6-8 weeks (for an initial transaction, with follow- on financings executed within a shorter time frame). As noted, it can be much faster to issue a private placement versus a public corporate bond (particularly for first¬time issuers) due to the elimination of prospectus drafting, rating agency diligence and registering requirements with the SEC.

Are Private Placement Programs/Trade Platforms Real or a Scam?

The first question we are usually asked is: are private placement programs (also known as PPPs) and trade platforms real or are they a scam? In short, they are real, but not in the way they are often described. There are many myths about these programs that we will attempt to dispel.

Perhaps the most common misconception regarding private placement programs and trade platforms is that they are the exclusive domain of the ultra-rich through secretive, invitation-only investments. Often, clients are told that they must pay large, upfront fees to gain access to these exclusive instruments. In addition, they are told they must submit POF (proof of funds), a CIS (client information summary) or KYC (know your client) package, along with their passport. Nothing could be further from the truth.

Private Placements Are Sometimes Bad Investments

A Private Placement Trading Program (PPP) is a lucrative way of investing and as long as the PPP is genuine, there is no financial risk for investors. As you can imagine, if you are offered a no-risk high profit opportunity in the stock market business you would probably be tempted to jump at the chance. However, if you are tempted by PPPs beware, and realize that they are not always what they seem. Many investors have been stung in PPP scams and billions of dollars have been lost. There are law suits underway, but they are notoriously slow to reach a conclusion and given the amount of scams that have been uncovered, relatively few perpetrators have gone to court.

High Returns for Ethical Investments

Private Placement Programs are those trading with Medium term Bank Notes (MTNs) or Treasury bills (T-Bills). They typically have a high return on the investment and are, more often than not associated with ethical trading. They involve programs which are humanitarian in nature. Investors are required to put part of their earnings into projects which are concerned with humanitarian, social or economic development. Profits from such projects go back into the economy, giving it a much-needed boost.

It is Not Legal for Financial Institutions to Invest in PPPs

Financial Institutions are not legally allowed to participate in such programs so have to find private individuals or companies to invest in them. The investor cannot lose money as the investment is underwritten by the trading group.

This means that the investor is in a win-win situation for once, so it is hardly surprising that some unethical companies have found PPPs useful for conning high level investors out of their capital. The difficulty is that every investor would love to invest in a PPP, but can't access them as they open and close quickly, so it is very difficult to find a performing trade.

Tell-Tale Signs That All is Not Well

When national brokerage firms refuse to touch Private Placement Programs, it's a sure sign that something is "rotten in the state of Denmark" to quote Shakespeare. Even with high commissions available and fees, PPPs are considered dangerous. It's a case of once bitten twice shy. Businesses have invested unethically in fields that they are not allowed to invest in under the terms of PPPs, including pornographic web sites. So now brokers are very wary of even considering a PPP.

Private Placements: SCAM or REAL?

They are REAL but like everything else you must do your research to make sure you are not getting yourself into a bad situation. Whether you feel the agent or principle disclosed everything about the company or investment strategy, do your own research in addition to the prospectus that is provided. Doubt everything until it is confirmed! I suggest that you deal with only reputable agents (now that's an oxymoron) or at least companies and syndicates that are visible and very assessable. That's important if you need to go "postal".

I personally only deal with organizations which I get to know the principles. In the mid-90s, I participated in a several private equities offering with USA

Technologies (OTC: USAA). Over the years since that period, management would invite me to participate usually packaging up a treasure trove of warrants and other hard to turn away from goodies. Regulon Global, a pharma focused on really innovative cancer drugs headquartered in Greece is a great opportunity for the long-term hold investors. I did a private placement investment to fuel their European clinical trials when they first developed their premier drug. I later tried brokering an acquisition deal with Wyeth Ayerst and GlaxoSmithKline but the Regulon CEO at the time got cold feet. It's hard to get some eggheads to see the bigger and more profitable picture at times.

When I was a venture capitalist, I learned that some people really just don't care about money. I personally don't trust anyone who doesn't care about money. I'm not saying I'd respect you more if you were some greedy little weasel but one shouldn't lose perspective of the benefits that money offers. If their actions and thoughts aren't contingent on making a dollar and they are motivated by something that is senseless or something you really can't identify, then who knows what they will do next.

Trading Platforms: SCAM or REAL?

REAL but watch out because there is an overwhelming number of scammers out there praying on anyone with a little green looking to double their savings and or retirement. The legitimate and performing trade platforms are very difficult to find out about. Noticed I said LEGITIMATE and

PERFORMING. The real deals are closely guarded secrets and participation is usually by invitation or association with the right uber rich financier. Those programs that you may have heard about from a guy who heard something from another guy or an obscure LinkedIn posting most likely ARE SCAMS.

At a minimum, it takes a $100 million to enter into a LEGITIMATE trade program. Any amount being marketed that is less than that is hopefully pooled by the platform's program manager until $100 million is reached. Why such a large amount in order to enter the trade? The tremendous profit spread could never be achieved without such sums being invested SUCCESSFULLY. This is why these "small cap" programs (anything under $150 million) market such generous profits to investors.

Very few programs exist that allow participation below $10 million. I have found a few platforms that do offer programs with a minimum investment of $50K to $2 million. The problem with the small cap programs is that they seldom last more than a few months before significantly raising the minimum investment or disappearing altogether.

If you are fortunate enough to possess the funds to invest in a trading platform, you must do your homework! Just because the broker or marketing materials mention that big name banks are involved someway in the deal means absolutely nothing. So what if the transactions are executed from the Bank of America Trading Desk. Knowing that doesn't make me feel any better about the risk. No matter how many controls may be in place to hedge risk, there is ALWAYS a chance that something may go wrong. There are strategies that you can do to reduce risk but make no mistake that small fraction of a half percent is still an element of risk.

Try to mitigate the risk of your investment vaporizing before your very eyes by first doing your research and getting verification that the people or organization you may do business with are who they say they are and that they possess all the necessary governing legal documents, regulatory filings and licenses to do what it is that they claim they do. All of these trading platforms operate and or are transacted off-shore due to strict US regulations. Just because the deal is off-shore doesn't mean that there aren't regulatory conditions and or mandatory filings in order to transact that type of business or service. If the platform is in China, verify that everything that all the "i"s are dotted and the "t"s are crossed per that Country's jurisdiction. If there are multiple jurisdictions involved within multiple countries VERIFY everything is of public record; trade licensing, corporate filings, assets under management, offers, etc.

While you are doing your homework, ask the agent or principle to provide proof that the program is performing. Copy of a SWIFTs is not proof of anything. Trading desk receipts are proof, paymaster escrow accounts verified are proof, etc. If the program doesn't offer it ask for non-depletion accounts that only YOU control and verify it with documentation. Also, ask for an insurance wrap on the funds. The wrap should also cover third-party allocations of funds. If they don't offer the insurance get a policy yourself. I can't stress it enough, verify EVERYTHING, especially what they claim and what is written in their contract. Make sure the contract addresses every possible situation including what happens if the program fails to perform. If so, aside from them hopefully and voluntarily returning your principle, try to negotiate some concessions for lost opportunities, interest, penalties, etc.

I know I most likely precluded you from investing in a trading platform, but at least you know the intense steps you must take to secure your money in the hands of potential criminals. Obviously, I have been around and have had both good and negative experiences with the program managers, agents, brokers, paymasters, etc. You have to stay on these S.O.B.s.

There are all types of trading platform structures; leveraged instruments, bank guarantees (BGs), escrow funding, leveraged loan financing, bullets, buy/sell, etc. Unless you can afford to potentially lose millions, I strongly suggest you invest in a "Buy/Sell" program for two reasons:

The risks are virtually non-existent if mitigated by some of the earlier suggestions; and they tend to be small cap programs requiring less capital to participate. The downside is that they typically don't pay the kinds of ridiculous returns as the others. Most small caps I have encountered pay a return between 8% to 10% monthly. Yes, monthly. Not bad if you are able to find a consistent performer. Generally, trading platform contracts are for one-year and do not auto-renew.

My first trading platform investment was a small cap gold buy/sell program where my funds were placed in a non-depletion escrow account and used as a proof of funds for buyers who wanted raw bullion directly from the mine. The agent representing the buyer would use the proof of funds to verify that the buyer is real and possesses the necessary cash deposit in order for the order to be filled. Once the order is filled, the bullion is delivered to the buyer COD. I received 10% monthly from that platform. After receiving returns like that for just providing the front money, I was hooked. I took my profits and jumped into a more sophisticated small cap program that paid out a 1000% in six months.

Unfortunately, not all the programs I invested in were as straight forward or successful. The good news is I actually made a nice return and to date have never lost my principle. The bad news is that two of the programs did not perform as marketed. The bottom-line is you must do your research and ask all the questions you can think of even the dumb ones.

CONCLUSION

Private placement trading programs are the opposite of public investments. Unlike public investing opportunities, only a small number of qualified people will be invited to invest privately in a company's business interests. From there, investing in private placement trading programs results in a profit for investors. The private transaction typically takes place between two parties and a middle facilitator. When it comes to all the investment opportunities that exist, this is truly one of the most lucrative options available to you. This kind of trading is based on the fractional reserve banking system, which is not a difficult concept to understand once you learn how it is tied to this kind of investing.

Once you have a clear understanding of what investing in this kid of programs involves and how fractional reserve banking comes into play, you must discover a way to get into a trading platform. This step near the beginning of the process can be the most difficult of all. This is because private placement trading is exactly that- private and secret. If you want to get involved with these programs or other alternative investment opportunities, you need to get in touch with an investing and trading company.

Getting started in investing in trading programs can yield huge returns. Placements typically start at more than $1 million and there is no cap as to how much you can invest. With this amount of money, you may be given estimates from brokers of unbelievable possibilities in return amounts. It may sound too good to be true, and it probably is. T o keep yourself from becoming greedy, you need to keep a realistic view on your investment and potential returns. Some opportunities may indeed yield incredible returns because this is a lucrative investment opportunity, but others many not meet up to your expectations. This is simply the nature of investing in private placement trading programs.

The best way to make money with trading programs is to find a genuine opportunity. The last thing you want, after all, is to be strung into a deal that ends up being illegal or illegitimate in some way. To spot an opportunity that you want to avoid, see if national brokerage firms refuse to become involved in the private placement program. When this happens, it may be the case that the brokerage firm has been bitten when investing in private placement trading programs before and they want to avoid a repeat occurrence.